William *Shakespeare*

AN ILLUSTRATED BIOGRAPHY

William Shakespeare

AN ILLUSTRATED BIOGRAPHY

Anthony Holden

LITTLE, BROWN & COMPANY

Boston • New York • London

A LITTLE, BROWN BOOK

FIRST PUBLISHED IN GREAT BRITAIN BY LITTLE, BROWN AND COMPANY IN 1999

THIS ABRIDGED ILLUSTRATED EDITION PUBLISHED IN GREAT BRITAIN BY
LITTLE, BROWN AND COMPANY IN 2002

A CIP CATALOGUE RECORD FOR THIS BOOK IS AVAILABLE FROM THE BRITISH LIBRARY.

ISBN 0 316 85159 0

DESIGNED BY ANDREW BARRON & COLLIS CLEMENTS ASSOCIATES
PRINTED AND BOUND IN SINGAPORE

LITTLE, BROWN AND COMPANY (UK)
BRETTENHAM HOUSE, LANCASTER PLACE, LONDON WC2E 7EN

FOR FRANK KERMODE

If my slight Muse do please these curious days,
The pain be mine, but thine shall be the praise.

Contents

Mrs. FITZWILLIAM as Mrs. PAGE.

"What! have I 'scap'd love-letters in the holiday time of my
beauty and am I now a subject for them? Let me see."
MERRY WIVES OF WINDSOR.
Act 2, Sc 1.

Prologue

There are no great biographies of Shakespeare, according to the American scholar Harold Bloom, 'not because we do not know enough, but because there is not enough to know'. Such resonant truths have never deterred well-meaning Bardolaters, both amateur and professional, from climbing on each other's shoulders to a height where the view is now as richly detailed as at any time since Shakespeare's own. But can we, amid the named and numbered trees of the Forest of Arden, espy the man?

Somewhere in the world, it is said, a book on Shakespeare is published every day. At the turn of the twenty-first century, as he is universally voted Man of the Millennium, and wins surrogate Oscars via the writers of the film *Shakespeare in Love*, Shakespeare is bigger business than ever. As his home town is increasingly colonized by tourists, whether or not they choose to visit the theatre which bears his name, the long-suffering son of Stratford is meanwhile being picked apart by historicists, feminists, Marxists, new historicists, post-feminists, deconstructionists, anti-deconstructionists, post-modernists, cultural imperialists and post-colonialists. Perhaps it is time someone tried to put him back together again.

This attempt claims no more than what the late Anthony Burgess called 'the right of every Shakespeare-lover who has ever lived to paint his own portrait of the man'. Burgess, to my mind, made the last, best attempt at a popular, accessible, yet academically sound biography — in 1970, a generation and more ago, now distant enough to justify yet another attempt by yet another generation to recreate the poet in its own metropolitan, turn-of-another-century image.

Four hundred years after the Globe first opened, Shakespeare's theatre is back on the south bank of the Thames for the first time since his own day, staging his plays in much the way his own audiences would have seen them. Four centuries since the long, glorious reign of the first Queen Elizabeth drew towards its close, England is approaching the Golden Jubilee of the second — an age when John of Gaunt's 'sceptr'd isle' is uncertain of its own identity, with

Scotland and Wales asserting their separateness within a potentially federal Europe, and Ireland still troubled, as compared with the first Elizabeth's mightily self-confident nation, pushing back the frontiers of science, culture and global exploration.

What more opportune moment to respond to Henry James's challenge by wielding 'the finer weapon, the sharper point, the stronger arm' in the pursuit of 'the more extended lunge'? My own motives and aspirations in tackling this most daunting of biographical tasks — beyond the chance to savour, in the happy phrase of my Oxford tutor, 'the apparently boundless hospitality of Shakespeare's imagination' — add up to a labour of love: an identikit portrait of a much-wanted man who appears to have spent his life and work wilfully trying to evade capture. 'We ask and ask,' as Matthew Arnold wrote of the man from Stratford. 'Thou smilest, and art still.'

In truth, as I maintain at the outset of this book, we know more about the life of Shakespeare than that of any of his literary contemporaries bar Ben Jonson. And the rest is there for all to see, in and between every line he ever wrote — as well as the order in which he wrote them. 'We do not understand Shakespeare from a single reading, and certainly not from a single play,' as T. S. Eliot sternly reminds us; but 'there is a relation between the various plays ... taken in order'. Yes, as even Eliot concedes, there is a 'pattern in Shakespeare's carpet'.

It is one of many oft-repeated 'Bardisms', fast approaching the status of cliché, that we do not read Shakespeare; he reads us. By the same token, continuing conflicts between the various factions of the booming Shakespeare industry suggest that too many academics no longer read Shakespeare so much as rewrite him. Is the same to be said of biographers?

Perhaps. But I must part company with Harold Bloom when he asserts that 'we cannot know, by reading Shakespeare and seeing him played, whether he had any extrapoetic beliefs or disbeliefs'. No writer, not even this *nonpareil*, can ever entirely absent himself from his work. Bloom takes G. K. Chesterton to task for suggesting that Shakespeare was a Catholic dramatist, and that Hamlet was 'more orthodox than sceptical'; yet he himself proceeds to counter-claim that 'by reading Shakespeare, I can gather that he did not like lawyers, preferred drinking to eating, and evidently lusted after both genders'.

As Bloom has also written elsewhere: 'If you read and re-read Shakespeare endlessly, you may not get to know either his character or his personality' — again, after the reading and re-reading that went into the writing of this book, I beg to differ — 'but you will certainly learn to recognise his temperament, his sensibility and his cognition.'

The arguments of both camps seem to me, as is so often the way with Shakespeare studies, equally legitimate, equally dubious. One scholar who has read this book in manuscript disagrees with some of it as violently as he 'rhapsodises' about the rest — depending, of course, on whether or not it supports his own, highly contentious point of view. Another eminent academic disapproves of the very concept of a Shakespeare biography, while a celebrated Shakespearean actor-cum-scholar generously says it has helped him to a better understanding of the works (which he knew pretty well in the first place).

To some lovers of Shakespeare, it is heresy to find biographical inferences between the lines of his poems and plays; to others, his true autobiography lies in his work. If the twain can never meet, it seems to me that there exists a middle ground through which it is relatively safe (and quite legitimate) to pick your way — a minefield, of course, sown with springes to catch not so much woodcocks as prodigal souls like mine, the blood burning, vows on the tip of the tongue, 'giving more light than heat', no doubt 'extinct in both'.

Mr Henry Betty as Faulconbridge, in 'King John'.
Engraved by George Hollis, 1792–1842.

One kindred spirit who sounds like he will forgive me the attempt, *pace* the outcome, is the novelist John Updike, who recently distilled the first 'and perhaps most worthy' reason for reading literary biographies as 'the desire to prolong and extend our intimacy with the author — to partake again, from another angle, of the joys we have experienced within this author's *oeuvre*, in the presence of a voice and mind we have come to love'.

Reading these words, in the midst of my task, made me realise that one reason I was writing this book was that I wanted to read it. Shakespeare biography has recently got so bogged down in disputes about the digging of ditches and mending of hedges, payment (or non-payment) of fines and tithes, the design and logistics of Elizabethan theatres, how his contemporaries brushed their teeth, whether they had bad breath, right down to the decor of the guest bedroom of an Oxford tavern where he may or may not have bedded the land-lord's wife – not to mention the perennial Fair Youths and Dark Ladies – that the man himself is too often allowed to slip away and watch from the wings, no doubt with a smirk, for whole chapters at a time. I have attempted to keep him squarely in sight, pin him firmly to the page, no matter how hard he has struggled to escape. It is fatal, I have found, to look away even for a moment. He is gone again, vanished to one of his own imaginary horizons. There follows the distant sound of cackling.

If each generation recreates Shakespeare in its own image, my contribution is to despatch him to the Lancashire of my (and, I am convinced, his) youth. As you read of young Will 'Shakeshafte' passing in his teens from the Hoghton family to the Hesketh household, you may or may not care to know that my late father was a shopkeeper in Hoghton Street, Southport, some twenty miles from the scene of these late-sixteenth-century events, and that one of the first young women on whom I looked with all Silvius' hopeless ardour for Phebe was a Hesketh, direct descendant of the local toffs who took in the young actor-play-wright in the 1580s. (Subsequently, since you ask, she married a publisher. Neither Shakespeare nor I can be expected to approve.)

Juvenilia apart, I must first acknowledge an obvious debt – spelt out in due detail in the source notes – to the four centuries of Shakespeare scholars and biographers who have gone before me, up to and including the present day. It is inevitable, in the words of a pioneer among the current crop, Ernst Honigmann, that 'everyone who writes about Shakespeare borrows from earlier writers'.

Alongside that of the late Sam Schoenbaum, greatest of twentieth-century Shakespeare archaeologists, of the buccaneering novelist-biographer Burgess, and of the iconoclastic Eric Sams, Honigmann's name heads the list of scholars whose work has helped to shape my own. (He has also been kind enough to read and evaluate a draft of my Chapters II and III.) But I have spared the reader a further list of my own extensive reading, as any Shakespeare bibliography worthy of the name would all but double the length of this book, which I have tried to keep within manageable bounds. So my research is itemised in the Source Notes, which offer publication details of the books I have found most rewarding. I have also chosen to spare the general reader the distraction of superscript note numbers in the text; the opening words of quotations may be found in the Source Notes, via page numbers in the running heads, to assist the reader towards original sources and further reading.

Quotations throughout the book conform primarily to the text of *The Riverside Shakespeare*, which I have found the most reliable, informative and scholarly single-volume edition of the Works. The Riverside text forms the basis of Professor Martin Spevack's computer-generated *Complete and Systematic Concordance to the Works of Shakespeare*, now abridged in the one-volume *Harvard Concordance to Shakespeare*. In all other quotations I have modernised the spelling, often with some reluctance, indulging myself by leaving an inconsistent few to retain their inalienable period charm.

The staff of the London Library and the Shakespeare Centre Library in Stratford-upon-Avon have been unfailingly helpful (as has Ben Holden, chasing down some of the more rarefied material in Oxford University's Bodleian and English faculty libraries). I am also grateful to the wide variety of academic Shakespeare specialists who have listened to and argued with me during my four years' work on this book; I will not drop their names here, as the responsibility for its contents should remain mine alone. The same goes for the many Shakespearean actors, directors and enthusiasts, both amateur and highly professional, who have shown great patience when buttonholed by the Ancient Mariner of Bardic lore into whom I have turned these last few years.

A. Alvarez, Melvyn Bragg, John Fortune and Peter O'Toole kindly read the manuscript in typescript and made many helpful suggestions. I have rarely enjoyed such profound disagreements with anyone as genially as with Eric

Sams, who also took my penultimate draft to pieces, and will strenuously protest at much of what remains – notably on such contentious issues as collaboration, 'memorial reconstruction', 'pirate' publication (with special reference to the Sonnets), right down to the spelling of the name of Shakespeare's only son. I am also grateful to Professors Richard Wilson and Richard Dutton of Lancaster University for an invitation to speak at the 'Lancastrian Shakespeare' conference in July 1999, held in part at Hoghton Tower, under the auspices of the university's Shakespeare programme; and to the many scholars present (notably Father Peter Milward, Professors Stephen Greenblatt, Eamonn Duffy, Gary Taylor and others) from whose wisdom and expertise I benefited.

MISS GLYN AS CLEOPATRA,
IN 'ANTONY AND CLEOPATRA'.
ENGRAVED BY GEORGE HOLLIS,
1792–1842.

The *Observer* generously gave me unlikely amounts of space to expatiate on Shakespeare in the various guises in which he continues to haunt all our lives; my thanks to its Review editor, Lisa O'Kelly, and arts editor, Jane Ferguson. Robert Butler, drama critic of the *Independent on Sunday*, kindly took me to many Shakespeare first nights, which also entailed many patient hours of argument. He of all people knows the travails that went into this book – beyond, of course, my wife and children, who have welcomed Shakespeare into our household with all the forbearance they have previously shown such long-stay guests as Laurence Olivier, Tchaikovsky and others, even the Prince of Wales.

The book would never have been written without the touching faith in my ability to do so of my friend and publisher, Alan Samson; I am equally grateful to Philippa Harrison, Andrew Gordon, Rosalie Macfarlane, Linda Silverman, Amanda Murray and all their colleagues at Little, Brown on both sides of the Atlantic, and to Julia Charles, Andrew Barron (design), Arianne Burnette (picture research) and Rachel Connolly (editor) for the painstaking care they have lavished on this illustrated edition. My agent, Gill Coleridge, has been her constant, supportive, inimitable self.

But my deepest debt ranges over thirty years, from my inspirational tutor in the late 1960s at Merton College, Oxford, John Jones, author of the wonderfully observed *Shakespeare at Work*, to my friend and mentor Sir Frank Kermode, whose lifetime steeped in the poetry of Shakespeare has now seen publication of his indispensable *Shakespeare's Language*. Such fun did Frank and I have while simultaneously writing about our mutually beloved Bard, if in different ways and at very different levels, pooling thoughts both wonderfully insightful (his) and outrageously erratic (mine), that it is as much a pleasure as a privilege to have wrung from him his leave for the dedication.

A NOTE ON MONETARY VALUES

The computer wizardry of Robin Marris, Emeritus Professor of Economics at Birkbeck College, London, suavely picked up my gauntlet by coming up with a mercifully simple formula for the approximate conversion of Elizabethan monetary values to those of the present day. Commodities such as foods must be excluded because prices would of course fluctuate according to their scarcity value. In the case of more stable figures, such as income, expenditure and property, the Marris formula works out simply as 'multiply by 500'.

Shakespeare's purchase of New Place in 1597 for £60, for instance, would convert to £30,000 at today's prices, which seems a bargain for one of the most handsome houses at the heart of a provincial town. His annual income from the theatre, which at its peak reached some £200, would thus be the equivalent of a handsome £100,000 — rather less, I am given to believe, than the annual income of some of the leading playwrights of our own day.

I
STRATFORD
1564–1569

William Shakespeare of Stratford-upon-Avon was to bring lasting lustre to a surname long held to be an embarrassment … Shakespeare survived as a fairly common surname in Warwickshire and its environs throughout the late Middle Ages, particularly in the thriving city of Coventry and a cluster of villages in what was then the Forest of Arden.

Both his parents were illiterate. His father, who rose to become Mayor of Stratford-upon-Avon, all his life signed his name with a mark. His mother, like most women of her day, was never taught to read or write.

Their son William's baptism was recorded in the parish register of Stratford's Holy Trinity Church on 26 April 1564. But there is no further evidence, alas, to support the popular belief that William Shakespeare was born — as fifty-two years later he was to die — on 23 April, the date celebrated in England since 1222 as the feast day of dragon-slaying St George. As the poet's posthumous fame grew, securing a unique niche for his country in the cultural history of the world, it was a natural enough temptation for posterity to unite the birthday of England's national poet with that of its patron saint. But the tradition is based on a false assumption, that Elizabethan baptisms invariably took place three days after the birth.

The instruction given to parents in the 1559 Prayer Book, five years before Shakespeare's birth, was to have the christening performed before the first Sunday or Holy Day following the birth 'unless upon a great and reasonable cause declared to the curate and by him approved'. In 1564 the 23rd day of April happened to fall on a Sunday, four days after the feast day of St Alphege and two before that of St Mark — traditionally an unlucky day, so the curate's permission to avoid it may well have been forthcoming.

But the contemporary inscription on Shakespeare's tomb in Holy Trinity — that same church where he was christened on 26 April by the vicar of the parish, John Bretchgirdle — reads that he died in his fifty-third year ('*obiit anno ... aetatis* 53'). We know that he died on St George's Day, 23 April, so this would seem to imply that he was born before it, however marginally. There are few more satisfactory resolutions of this problem than that of the poet Thomas de Quincey, who suggested that Shakespeare's granddaughter Elizabeth Hall married on 22 April 1626 'in honour of her famous relation' — choosing the sixty-second anniversary of his birth, in other words, rather than the tenth of his death.

William Shakespeare of Stratford-upon-Avon was to bring lasting lustre to a surname long held to be an embarrassment. In 1487, on becoming a celibate

(PAGE 16)
PEG WOFFINGTON AS
ROSALIND WITH CELIA
AND TOUCHSTONE IN THE
FOREST OF ARDEN, FROM
'AS YOU LIKE IT'.
PAINTING ATTRIBUTED TO
FRANCIS HAYMAN,
1708–76.

don at Merton College, Oxford, one Hugh Shakespeare had changed his name to Hugh Sawnders. '*Mutatum est istud nomen eius, quia vile reputatum est,*' records the College Register: 'He changed that name of his, because of its base repute.' For all its ripe phallic imagery, shared with similar names like Shakestaff and Wagstaff, Shakespeare survived as a fairly common surname (in all manner of different spellings) in Warwickshire and its environs throughout the late Middle Ages, particularly in the thriving city of Coventry and a cluster of villages in what was then the Forest of Arden, a dozen miles north of Stratford-upon-Avon. In 1284 a William Sakspere of Clopton, Gloucestershire, was hanged for theft; a century later, in 1385, another William Shakespeare served on a coroner's jury in Balsall.

Between 1530 and 1550 tenant farmers called Richard Shakspere, Shakespere, Shakkespere, Shaxpere and Shakstaff were penalised on numerous occasions for non-attendance at the manor court at Warwick, choosing to pay the 2d fine rather than lose a day's work making the six-mile walk each way. In

CLOPTON BRIDGE.
ENGRAVING FROM A
DRAWING BY SAMUEL
IRELAND, 1795.

fact, of course, they were all the same man: the poet's grandfather, a tenant farmer in the village of Snitterfield, four miles north-east of Stratford on the main Warwick road. Richard Shakespeare's landlord was Robert Arden, of the nearby village of Wilmcote, in the parish of Aston Cantlow, whose daughter Mary would marry his son John in 1557. John was the second, perhaps the third of Richard's sons. Born in 1529, he was dubbed *agricola*, or husbandman, in documents relating to his father's estate; but by then, the early 1560s, he had long forsaken the traditional Shakespeare life on the land for what he saw as more prosperous urban pastures. Though raised in the family business of tenant-farming, John set his sights higher from early youth, migrating to the thriving market town of Stratford by the mid-point of the century.

Settled in a lush, wooded valley, by then a decent-sized town of some 1,500 souls, Stratford-upon-Avon originally took its name from the point where a Roman road (or 'straet') crossed (or 'forded') the elegant river flowing through its heart. One of the oldest settlements in Christian England, Stratford is mentioned in the Domesday Book as the personal fiefdom of the Bishops of Worcester; by Shakespeare's day its agricultural tenants had won their emancipation, and formed the nucleus of a thriving mercantile community, with artisans and shopkeepers displaying their wares on market days alongside the usual livestock and country produce. Already the Avon (Welsh for 'river') was spanned, as still it is, by a handsome stone bridge built by Sir Hugh Clopton, a wealthy local mercer who had risen to become Lord Mayor of London. In the heart of Stratford, in the last decade of the fifteenth century, Clopton built himself the biggest house in town, which he called New Place. It was one measure of the subsequent success in London of another son of Stratford, the

A PERSPECTIVE VIEW OF THE NEW PLACE.
DRAWING BY JOHN JORDAN, 1793.

(OPPOSITE)
STUDY FOR KING LEAR.
PAINTED BY JOSHUA
REYNOLDS, C.1760

WARWIC=
LECESTRIÆQ3
Comitat·, Ciuitat·
oppidorū, Villaru·
fluminū· Ceterarumq3
rerum omnium in
eisdem memorabi:
lium· noua· Veraq3
descriptio·

OCCIDENS

PARTE OF STAFFORDE SHIRE

PART·

SHI

PART OF SALOP Hales ouen SHIRE

Industria naturam ornat

PESTIS PATRIÆ PIGRICIL

PARTE OF WORCESTER SHIRE

PARTE OF GLOCESTER SHIRE

LYCHFELD
Fisheric
Elford
Whittenton
Corebro·ford
TAMEWORTH
Borne sta·
Wesford
Ammynton
Shenstou
Hynte
Villncote
Rushall
Aldridge
Drac
bassey
Hole
Barr
Myddleton
Sutton cofeld
Newhall
Moxhall
Kinsbur
Hamsted
Ker
Curdworth
Nether Whr
Sandwall
Wshawe
Mak
Handsworth
Yarneton hall
sh·hall·Wateterton
Shistoke
Pecyhall
Makesoke east
Aston
Castlebramy·che·
Ouldbury
Smethik
Dudson·hall
Ringeshurst
COLESHIL
BROMYCH·W
Edgebason
Yardley
W
Makesoke
Horborn
Sheldon
Packinton
Mon·f
Cole flu·
Helmedon
Brykenhull
Packinton ma·
Rea flu·
SOLYHVIL
Hampton
Mon·
Kyngesnorton
Heywood
Bayston
Barkeswell
Costen
Londonhall
Kuoll
The temple of
Quen·
bals·hall
Wytho Papell
W
Packwood
Hunn·sley
Arrow flu·
Alchurche
Nuthurst
Baddesley
Kenst
Tardbik
Howellgrange
Byrster
Skiltes
Tanworth
Lapworth
Roxhall
Wolodow
Ipsley
Beler
Rownton
Moseley
Feckenhm forest
Preston
Hatton
Grove Budbr
Feckenhm
Studley
Morton
Oulbarron
Clyverdon
Prior
Lampton
Sparnoll
Ounall
Norton
Anne lodge
HENLEY
Sherborn
Coighton
Asne
S
Wolston
Edson
Wuluardington
Brachin court
Kynnerton
Aston
Bearley
Smitersfeld
Inkbarrow
Arrow
Woolston
Busstepton
Morton
Rayler
AVLCESTER
Hasseler
Bessey
Busshopton
Clapton
Charleston
Wetheley
Loxhall
Whyesford
Morehall
Grasson
Draton
Autton
STREFFORD
Rouselinche
Bowinton
Bicford
Byrnton
Laddinton
Walton
Abbot merton·
Broone
Goldcote
Harryngton
Sawford
Wylsford
Milcote
Atherton
Doffynton
Preston
Aldermaston
Bullenmarsh
Auon flu·
Cleve
Pelworth
Marton sickwar
Over eatenton
Carleton
N·Lynleton
Uffenton
Brode marston
Whitchurche
Newbo
Nether
Oure
Belle
Quynreton
Haveforde
EVESHOLME
Myckleton
Stoke
Hanston
Fredenton
Whattcote
Tydecote
Tysoes
Blackwell
Humpton
Dorsingscote
Campton
Windrston
CAMPDEN
SHIPSTON
Bache Brider
Ebberton
Tilmorney
Glocester
shire
Stratton
Burmyngton
Pesford
Worces·
Honyngston·
Ichinton
Weston
Blocker
Lemyngton
Cherinton
Morton hynmar·she
Byrton on the heath
Whichford
Eastrude
The foure Shire stones
Lange compton
Worcester shire
Comptone
Glocester shire
MER

Map of Warwickshire, from Christopher Saxton's 'Atlas of England and Wales', c.1579.

glover's boy William Shakespeare, that eventually he in turn would become the proud owner of New Place.

A hundred miles from the capital, but handily close to the major Midlands townships of Worcester and Warwick, Banbury and Oxford, Stratford was described by a contemporary map-maker as *'emporium non inelegans'* – a market town not without its charms, already boasting the handsome thirteenth-century parish church of the Holy Trinity, and the smaller but even older, equally finely-detailed chapel of the Guild of the Holy Cross.

THE MARKET HOUSE, SITE OF THE MARKET CROSS,
STRATFORD-UPON-AVON. UNKNOWN ARTIST.

We know that by 1552 John Shakespeare was living on the north-eastern side of town, in Henley Street, thanks to his ignominious debut in the town records on 29 April: fined a shilling, along with Humphrey Reynolds and Adrian Quiney, for making an unauthorised dunghill – *sterquinarium*, or midden heap – in front of the house of a neighbour, the wheelwright William Chambers. In those days of the plague, a fine equivalent to two days' pay for an artisan was a suitably stern judgement on those too idle to use the communal muck-hill at the rural end of the street. In a rare defiance of the family tradition (and his own later practice), John Shakespeare paid his fine promptly. Already, it seems, he had it in mind to become not just a worthy citizen of Stratford, but a civic eminence. This early misdemeanour appears to have proved no bar to his upward mobility.

After serving (we can but assume) the statutory seven-year apprenticeship, Shakespeare's father had entered trade as a glover and whittawer: a dresser of 'whitleather', soft light-coloured leather. Between 1556 and 1592 various legal documents concerning unpaid debts and bail sureties unambiguously describe Johannes Shakyspere, or Shakspere, or Shackspeare, as a 'glover'. His craft

(OPPOSITE)
HAMLET AND HORATIO
IN THE CEMETERY.
DRAWING WITH
WATERCOLOUR BY
EUGENE DELACROIX,
1799–1863.

involved the 'tawing' of hides and skins — of deer and horses, goats and sheep, but not protected livestock such as cattle or pigs — by soaking them in a solution of salt and alum (aluminium sulphate). The resulting leathers he fashioned not only into gloves, but belts, purses, aprons — whatever he could sell in his shop, or in the glovers' stall given prime position on market days beneath the clock of Stratford's Market Cross, today the traffic island at the junction of the High Street, Bridge Street and Henley Street, which leads to the Shakespeare Memorial Theatre.

The seventeenth-century diarist John Aubrey, one of the first to visit Stratford in search of Shakespeare evidence, reported unequivocally that the poet's father was a butcher. Aubrey is never the most reliable of witnesses, but it does seem plausible, in the light of later events, that there was a period in John Shakespeare's life when he might have defied the regulations strictly separating the otherwise allied professions of whittawer and butcher. He certainly traded openly in the wool of sheep slaughtered for their skins. The eastern wing of the Henley Street house which doubled as his leather goods store was known as 'the Woolshop'; when the floor was relaid in the nineteenth century, after the house had become an inn, the landlord testified to finding beneath the floorboards 'the remnants of wool, and the refuse of wool-combing … imbedded with the earth of the foundation.'

R: Greene del.

The House in Stratford upon Avon in which Shakespeare was born.

'THE BIRTHPLACE'.
THE HOUSE IN STRATFORD-UPON-AVON IN
WHICH SHAKESPEARE WAS BORN.

So why not their meat as well, if under-the-counter, hugger-mugger? According to Aubrey, the young William himself would kill a calf 'in a high style, & make a speech'; and there are plenty of expert references to the art of butchery in the plays. Other legal documents, the key pieces of our jigsaw for this period, involve John Shakespeare in suits concerning the sale and purchase of timber, and barley, whose sole commercial use was for the manufacture of

(OPPOSITE)
LADY MACBETH.
PAINTING BY JOHANN
HEINRICH FÜSSLI,
1741–1825.

beer and ale. Clearly he was something of an entrepreneur, a jack of all trades — a '*Johannes factotum*', as his son was enviously to be mocked, during his father's lifetime. John Shakespeare, again like his son after him, was also something of a property dealer.

If by 1552 Shakespeare's father owned or rented all or part of the Henley Street house still held sacred (despite scant evidence) as The Birthplace, he soon added to his property portfolio with the purchase in 1556 of a freehold estate with garden and croft, *tenementum cum gardino et crofto*, in Greenhill Street (later to become known as More Towns End). The business must have been thriving, for that same year also saw him buy an adjacent house in Henley Street, complete with garden, which would become the east wing or Woolshop when the two properties were joined together as a handsome, three-gabled dwelling.

More than forty years on, in 1597, the Stratford records show John selling off a narrow strip of land alongside this property to a draper named George Badger, for the purpose of building a wall, and another small parcel to Edward Willis of King's Norton, who proposed to open an inn called the Bell. Thus we can be reasonably sure that Henley Street remained the Shakespeare family home, through many vicissitudes for its paterfamilias, over half a century and more. It was still in the family 150 years later.

In 1553, soon after John Shakespeare had settled there, the borough of Stratford-upon-Avon had received its formal charter of incorporation from the Crown. Subject to the whims of the lord of the manor — in this case the Earl of Warwick, who still nominated the vicar and schoolmaster, and had power of veto over the borough's choice of bailiff, or mayor — this afforded a large degree of self-government to an elected council of aldermen and burgesses, who themselves appointed lesser functionaries. As luck would have it, the ambitious glover had arrived in the right town at the right time, the perfect moment to establish a mercantile foothold in the community while answering its new need for civic leaders. Nor, presumably, would a badge of office — and thus local respectability — be all that bad for business.

John's first recognition came in September 1556, within three years of the borough's incorporation, when he was chosen as one of its two ale-tasters — an office for 'able persons and discreet', whose duties were to check that bakers made loaves of regulation weight, and brewers 'wholesome' ales and beers at regulation prices. The ale-taster's powers were considerable: those he found in breach of the regulations were liable to appear before the twice-yearly manorial court, or 'leet', which had the power to inflict punishments from fines to a whipping, a sojourn in the stocks or pillory, or even worse public humiliation in the 'cucking stool' — a chair in the shape of a giant chamber-pot, in which the offender was ducked in the river to the delighted derision of his clientele.

Within nine months of his appointment, in June 1557, the new ale-taster found himself on the wrong side of the law, blotting his copybook by failing to attend three sittings of the Court of Record in his official capacity. The 8d fine he paid seems to have been worth it, for that spring saw John Shakespeare with other priorities to take his mind off his duties.

The journey back and forth to Wilmcote, presumably after hours, would have taken its toll on John's extra-curricular activities. Having established a secure base in the heart of Stratford, he returned to his rural roots for his bride, while still intent on social advancement. Mary Arden was not just the daughter of a prosperous farmer, his father's landlord; hers was one of Warwickshire's most prominent families, tracing its ancestry back beyond the Norman Conquest to the Domesday Book, fully four columns of which were filled by the landholdings of Turchill of Arden — more than any other individual.

Mary was the youngest of eight daughters of the widowed Robert Arden, whose second marriage in April 1548 (to Agnes Hill, née Webbe, widow of another prosperous farmer) added four stepchildren to the substantial brood already crammed into the two-storey Wilmcote farmstead. Whether it was the timber-frame house in Featherbed Lane identified in the late eighteenth century, and today visited by flocks of tourists, as 'Mary Arden's home', we cannot be sure — any more than we can be sure that her son William was born in the Henley Street manse today held sacred as 'The Birthplace'. But it would have been very similar, with its stone foundation and gabled dormers, timbered ceilings and rough-hewn oak beams, stone hearths and inglenooks, its main walls bedecked with painted hangings.

No record survives of John Shakespeare's marriage to Mary Arden, but it must have taken place — presumably in the parish church of St John the Baptist, Aston Cantlow, where no register was yet kept — towards the end of 1557. Their first child was born in the ninth month of 1558; but Mary would not have married during 1556, as her father lay dying. On 24 November that year Robert Arden made his will, whose terms suggest that his youngest daughter was, like King Lear's, also his favourite. Beyond the customary ten marks, Mary's father left her his most valuable possession in its entirety: the Arden estate in Wilmcote, named Asbies, 'and the crop upon the ground sown and tilled as it is'.

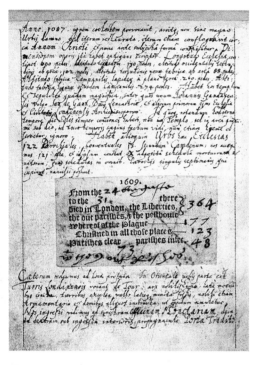

A PLAGUE BILL IN A SMALL PRINTED FORM OF 1609,
WITH SPACE FOR LISTING WEEKLY MORTALITIES.

Such was the handsome dowry Mary Arden brought to her marriage to the Stratford glover, by whom she would bear eight children in all — four sons and four daughters — over twenty years. A decade or so older than his wife, John would live into his seventies, well beyond the average span of his day, and Mary would outlive him by some seven years.

William was the third of their children to be born, but the first to live beyond childhood. A daughter, Joan, had been christened on 15 September 1558 by Roger Dyos, a Catholic priest driven from his post soon after Queen Elizabeth succeeded her Catholic half-sister Mary on the throne later that year. No record has been found of poor Joan's death or burial; but the fact that the Shakespeares christened another daughter by the same name eleven years later, on 15 April 1569, amounts to melancholy proof that the first Joan did not

(OPPOSITE)
HAMLET. PAINTING BY
GUSTAVE-ADOLPHE
MOSSA.

survive childhood, probably dying at the age of only one or two, as the register for the years 1559–60 is particularly sketchy. A second daughter, Margaret, was baptised on 2 December 1562 by the newly arrived Anglican priest, John Bretchgirdle, who also performed her funeral only four months later, in April 1563.

The Shakespeares' third child was himself lucky to survive infancy. William was less than three months old when the plague struck Stratford, imported from the slums of London by itinerant traders and vagabonds. '*Hic incepit pestis*' reads the dread entry in the burial register for 11 July 1564, beside the name of Oliver Gunne, an apprentice – only the twentieth person to be interred since 1 January, compared with 240 during the remaining five months of the year. It is a fair estimate that more than 200 souls – or one in seven of Stratford's population – were carried off by the grim disease, those most at risk being the community's youngest and oldest members. The records show that the plague claimed all four children of the Green family, neighbours of the Shakespeares in Henley Street. It seems highly likely that Mary, having already lost two daughters in their infancy, would have evacuated her firstborn son to the safety of her family home at Wilmcote, still occupied by her widowed stepmother, for the duration.

Already a burgess, an elected member of the council, her husband attended an emergency meeting that August, held alfresco to avoid the dangers of contagion. John Shakespeare contributed three shillings to a fund to assist victims of the plague, which did not abate until December, with the onset of the midwinter cold. By then, the turn of the year 1564–65, Shakespeare's father was a rising star of the Stratford council chamber.

On 30 September 1558, two weeks after the birth of his first child, the well-married glover had been sworn in (with Humphrey Plymley, Roger Sadler and John Taylor) as one of the borough's four constables, 'able-bodied citizens charged with preserving the peace'. Although proverbially stupid – an Elizabethan tradition his son would immortalise in the characters of Constables Dogberry and Dull – these local worthies, guardians of law and order, took on unenviable responsibilities in these unruly times. John Shakespeare would often have been called upon to break up drunken brawls, confiscate weapons from men made menacing by liquor, and give evidence against them in court. He was also responsible for policing the town's precautions against the ever-present threat of fire, and reporting to the church authorities any malingerers caught 'bowling, gaming or tippling' when they should have been at divine worship.

For a year Shakespeare's father evidently performed these duties efficiently enough, for 6 October 1559 saw him reappointed 'petty constable' – despite a fine that April for 'failing to keep his gutter clean' – and promoted to the equally unpopular role of '*affeeror*', or 'assessor', the civic functionary responsible for assessing fines not laid down by statute. It was not long before his upward progress reached its first plateau, with his election as one of Stratford's fourteen burgesses, the bulk of the town council responsible for all administration, who met in the Guild Hall every morning at 9 AM.

Whatever the effect of his public duties on the conduct of his business, John Shakespeare's fluctuating financial fortunes seem at first to have had little impact on his civic standing. His three-shilling contribution to the plague fund in the August following William's birth was followed by only sixpence the following month, at the end of which his name enters the municipal lists as a

JUBILEE AT STRATFORD,
1764.
UNKNOWN ARTIST.

witness to a corporation order. Already he was the Borough Treasurer, a regular attender of council meetings, who presented Stratford's annual accounts for 1564 at a plenary meeting held on 1 March 1565. By July he had been elevated to Alderman — unembarrassed, it seems, by an order shortly thereafter to pay £3 2s 7d 'for a restitution of an old debt'. In mid-February 1566 the records show him again presenting the annual accounts, a citizen solid enough to stand bail that September for one Richard Hathaway — father, as it happens, of his son's future bride. Each time he 'signed' the borough accounts, Shakespeare's father used as his mark an elegantly drawn pair of compasses, one of the tools of his trade.

As the Shakespeare family prospered, so it grew. A second son, Gilbert, was christened on 13 October 1566; like William he managed to survive infancy, living until 1612. Named after John Shakespeare's friend Gilbert Bradley, a fellow glover and council member, Gilbert Shakespeare appears to have followed his brother to London, where he is described in 1597 as a haberdasher of St Bride's, before returning to Stratford, where he seems to have fallen into undesirable company and occasionally foul of the law. The record of his burial, on 3 February 1612, four years before William, shows that he died *adolescens*, or unmarried.

In September 1567 we find their father being addressed for the first time as 'Mr Shakespeyr', a title of some considerable dignity. Another year, and he has been elected bailiff, or mayor, in his mid-thirties, in a three-way contest with Robert Perrot and Robert Salisbury held on 4 September 1568. On 1 October John presided over his first council meeting as bailiff, and five days later over his first Court of Record. As an impressionable four-year-old, the future playwright would now see a po-faced clutch of mace-bearing sergeants arrive at Henley Street early each day to escort his fur-trimmed father, with great ceremony, in a procession through the streets of Stratford to preside over the morning meetings at the Guild Hall. On Thursdays and fair-days the same parade would snake through the market and the fair, and on Sundays process solemnly to church, where the Shakespeare family now sat in the front pew. As bailiff, John Shakespeare shared with one other senior alderman the duties of Justice of the Peace: issuing warrants, hearing cases of debt and local by-law violations, negotiating with the lord of the manor. On Thursdays, after market, he would set the price of corn, and thus of bread and ale, for the following week, amid furious lobbying from bakers and brewers.

With civic honours came further commercial prosperity. On 4 November 1568 Mayor Shakespeare sold five hundredweight of wool to John Walford of Marlborough – a debt he was still pursuing more than thirty years later; and in 1568–70 he was recorded as the tenant of Ingon Meadow, a fourteen-acre estate two miles north-east of Stratford, in the parish of Hampton Lucy.

As his worldly success spread to the countryside of his and Mary's roots, to the very land farmed by his wayward brother Harry, John stepped down from Stratford's top job, choosing not to exercise his right to run for another term of office. Most likely, having achieved all he could by way of civic eminence, he deemed it more than time to return his attention to the family business. But he remained a respected elder of Stratford, his advice valued by the corporation, who in September 1571 elected him Chief Alderman and Justice of the Peace for the coming year, and ex-officio deputy to the new bailiff, his old friend and Henley Street neighbour Adrian Quiney, a mercer. In January 1572 the two rode together to London as ambassadors for the borough, deputed by their fellow councillors to report on parliamentary affairs affecting Stratford and represent its interests 'according to their discretions'.

During 1569, the year of the birth of the second Joan, John Shakespeare had mustered all his confidence to describe himself as 'Bailiff, Justice of the Peace, the Queen's Officer and Chief of the Town of Stratford' in his formal application to the College of Arms for the ultimate in self-made respectabil-ity: a coat of arms. This outward sign of his worldly success would set the seal, literally, on two decades of solid achievement.

But it was not to be – not, at any rate, for another quarter of a century, until his increasingly successful playwright son reapplied on his father's behalf in 1596 to the College of Arms, then as now on the banks of the Thames at Blackfriars, directly opposite the Globe Theatre. Then, at last, the Clarenceux King-of-Arms duly noted that John Shakespeare 'was a magistrate in Stratford upon Avon. A justice of the peace, he married a daughter and heir of Arden, and was good of substance and habileté'. But this first application in 1569 was declined by the authorities in London – for reasons which are nowhere documented, if not difficult to surmise.

John Shakespeare's eldest son had been born in dangerous times. It was less than half a century since the Queen's father, King Henry VIII, had broken with Rome, despoiled and looted church landholdings and shrines, executed notables from Sir Thomas More to two of his own wives, including Elizabeth's mother.

The Elizabethan era was approaching its apogee – a sustained period of military, political, scientific and cultural achievement without parallel in British history. It was also an age of ferocious religious persecution. Herself a deeply devout and civilised woman, Elizabeth presided with apparent reluctance over the pursuit, torture and execution of papists, in sporadic purges of varying intensity. But it was a time for followers of the 'old' faith to tread carefully, to worship in corners – if necessary, to deny their faith or at the least 'equivocate'.

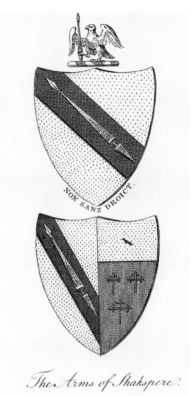

The Arms of Shakspere.

SHAKESPEARE'S COAT OF ARMS.
UNATTRIBUTED ENGRAVING
PUBLISHED IN 1787.

In 1757, a century and a half after John Shakespeare's death, a document of great significance was found hidden in the rafters of the family house in Henley Street – by then occupied by Thomas Hart, a direct lineal descendant of William's sister Joan. Retiling Hart's roof was a team of workmen led by Joseph Moseley, a master-builder described as 'very honest, sober, industrious', who on 29 April came upon a small 'paper-book', or pamphlet, tucked between the old tiling and the rafters. Its six stitched leaves turned out to contain fourteen articles amounting to a profession of Roman Catholic faith.

The document, which has become known as John Shakespeare's Spiritual Last Will and Testament, passed from Hart and Moseley to a local alderman, on to the eighteenth-century Shakespeare reliquary John Jordan and eventually (via the vicar of Stratford, James Davenport) to Shakespeare's eighteenth-century biographer, Edmund Malone. Having satisfied himself that it was genuine, though by now lacking its first page, Malone duly published it as an appendix to his 1790 edition of the Works.

The document has since vanished, depriving the advanced techniques of modern scholarship of the chance to address questions regarding the script, the paper, the watermark, the handwriting and, of course, John Shakespeare's signature. Was it a cross or his characteristic mark of the glover's compass? Malone subsequently recanted his conviction that the document was genuine, and the hapless Jordan was accused of forgery; it took until 1923 for a diligent Jesuit scholar, burrowing around the British Museum, to come up with an uncannily similar Italian document, also dating from the sixteenth century.

This was the 'last testament' of Saint Carlo Borromeo, the Cardinal Archbishop of Milan, who died in 1584 and was canonized in 1610. Borromeo's 'Last Will of the Soul, made in health for the Christian to secure himself from the temptations of the devil at the hour of death' was composed during a virulent bout of the plague in Milan in the 1570s, said to have claimed 17,000 Catholic lives. His Testament, which became a mantra of the Counter-Reformation, was clearly the original of the English translation found hidden in what once had been John Shakespeare's roof.

How did it get there? In 1580 Borromeo was visited in Milan by a group of Jesuit missionaries, led by Father Edmund Campion, an English recusant who two years later would be tried and gruesomely executed for treason. Campion and his colleagues brought back with them to England copies of Borromeo's testament, which was now circulating around Catholic Europe in huge quantities. 'Three or four thousand or more of the Testaments' were ordered from Rome by Campion and his colleagues, 'for many persons desire to have them.' Once back in England, Campion passed through the Midlands – specifically Lapworth, just twelve miles from Stratford – en route to Lancashire, where he was again to play a significant role in the life of young William Shakespeare.

Campion's host at Lapworth was Sir William Catesby, a relative by marriage of the Ardens, who was arrested and imprisoned in the Fleet for his pains. In Elizabethan England, Catholics literally risked their lives by admitting popish priests into their houses, whether to take their confession and celebrate Mass or merely to indulge in theological discussion. Policed by the Privy Council, who conducted periodic raids on secret strongholds of

EDMUND CAMPION.
ENGRAVING BY J. NEEFS.

recusancy all over the country, adherence to the 'old' faith was a crime amounting to treason, and punishable by death. Elizabeth's reign saw almost 200 Catholics meet excruciating ends on the public scaffold. Just two years after her own death, Catholic apostasy reached its celebrated climax in the 1605 'Powder Treason', now better known as 'the Gunpowder Plot' – whose leader was not Guy Fawkes, as 5 November legend would have it, but Robert Catesby, son of that same Sir William who invited Edmund Campion to visit Warwickshire in 1581.

An English translation of Borromeo's Testament, which finally came to light as recently as 1966, proved that the document faithfully attested by John Shakespeare was thus formulaic, but genuine beyond all doubt. A lifelong recusant – as witnessed by his subsequent fines for non-attendance of church, even while still a prominent member of the Stratford community – Shakespeare's father might well have been one of the furtive souls invited by Catesby, his Catholic wife's Catholic kinsman, to meet Campion at Lapworth, and to carry away one of the secretly-made English translations imported by the thousand from Rome. If not, it was probably passed to him by John Cottom, then the Stratford schoolmaster, whose recusant brother Thomas was one of Campion's travelling companions.

Three years later, a new round of raids and persecution dogged Warwickshire Catholics after a rash attempt by a deranged local fundamentalist, John Somerville, to assassinate the Queen. As the authorities descended in search of vengeance, the clerk of the council, Thomas Wilkes, bore witness to the urgent efforts of local recusants to 'clear their houses of all show of suspicion'. Somerville, who was captured and hanged en route to London, was married to Margaret Arden, a Catholic cousin of Shakespeare's mother. Perhaps this was the moment her husband felt it prudent to hide his copy of the Spiritual Testament up in the roof?

Seventeen when the Testament came into the family home, and twenty by the time his father felt obliged to hide it, the precocious William certainly seems to have absorbed its contents, whatever his personal reaction to them. The Testament's Item I acknowledged the possibility of being 'cut off in the blossom of my sins', a terrifying prospect catered for in Item IV: 'I, John

Shakespeare, do protest that I will also pass out of this life, armed with the last sacrament of extreme unction: the which if through any let or hindrance I shall not be able to have, I do now also for that time demand and crave the same.' The words of the English translation find a direct echo in those of the Ghost of Hamlet's Father, written within a year of the death of the poet's; no shriving time allowed, the Ghost of Hamlet's Father occupies an authentically Catholic version of Purgatory.

Shakespeare's Catholic indoctrination in childhood ran deep, whatever the subsequent falling-off in his beliefs. For both father and son, throughout the poet's youth, the 'equivocation' so dear to the heart of the Porter in *Macbeth* was a necessary evil to survive amid the religious McCarthyism then dogging Warwickshire dissenters.

THE GUNPOWDER PLOT CONSPIRATORS, 1605.
UNKNOWN ARTIST.

By the time he felt obliged to hide his Catholic Testament in the roof at Henley Street, Shakespeare's father was retired from active local politics, and celebrating the birth of his first grandchild by his son William. How it must have pained him, twenty years earlier, to fulfil his duties as Stratford's chamberlain by authorising the payment of two shillings to workmen charged with the task of 'defacing images in the chapel' — Stratford's Guild Chapel, embellished with papist murals of the murder of Thomas à Becket, St Helena's Dream and the Day of Judgement — and hitherto protected by the most powerful man in town, William Clopton, and his son, both Catholics.

But Clopton senior had died in 1560, and now his son had taken himself abroad. Given the political climate, the local council seized the moment to mutilate the heretical frescoes, in danger of bringing into disrepute a town so recently granted its royal charter. Two years later the council spent a further two shillings on the cost of dismantling the chapel's rood loft. And in 1571,

John Shakespeare was present when his friend and successor as bailiff, Adrian Quiney, ordered the replacement of the chapel's stained-glass windows with clear panes, and the disposal of the popish capes and vestments still preserved in the Chapel, if long since disused.

John Shakespeare may have disguised his religion well enough during his rise to civic eminence, like many fellow Catholics at that time of persecution. But this was an age of informers, well paid for their pains, who helped the authorities keep a close eye on countless pockets of papist defiance throughout the land. John's semi-concealed religious sympathies may well have been responsible for the College of Arms's otherwise mysterious refusal to grant him a coat of arms in 1569. They may also have played a role in the sudden, unwelcome development — eventually to cut short the education of his five-year-old schoolboy son William — that over the next few years, after two decades of sustained success, the former Mayor of Stratford's fortunes went into an abrupt and quite unexpected decline.

(BELOW)
SHAKESPEARE'S BIRTHPLACE IN THE MID-NINETEENTH CENTURY. UNKNOWN ARTIST.
(PAGES 42–43)
OPHELIA, FROM 'HAMLET', 1852. PAINTING BY JOHN EVERETT MILLAIS, 1829–96.

✝ A a b c d e f g h i j k l m n o p q
r ſ s t u v w x y z & a e i o u
A B C D E F G H I J K L M N O P Q
R S T U V W X Y Z.

a e i o u | a e i o u
ab eb ib ob ub ba be bi bo bu
ac ec ic oc uc ca ce ci co cu
ad ed id od ud da de di do du

In the Name of the Father, & of the
Son, & of the Holy Ghoſt. *Amen.*

OUR Father, which art in
Heaven, hallowed be thy
Name; thy Kingdom come, thy
Will be done on Earth, as it is in
Heaven. Give us this Day our
daily Bread; and forgive us our
Treſpaſſes, as we forgive them
that Treſpaſs againſt us: And
lead us not into Temptation, but
deliver us from Evil. *Amen.*

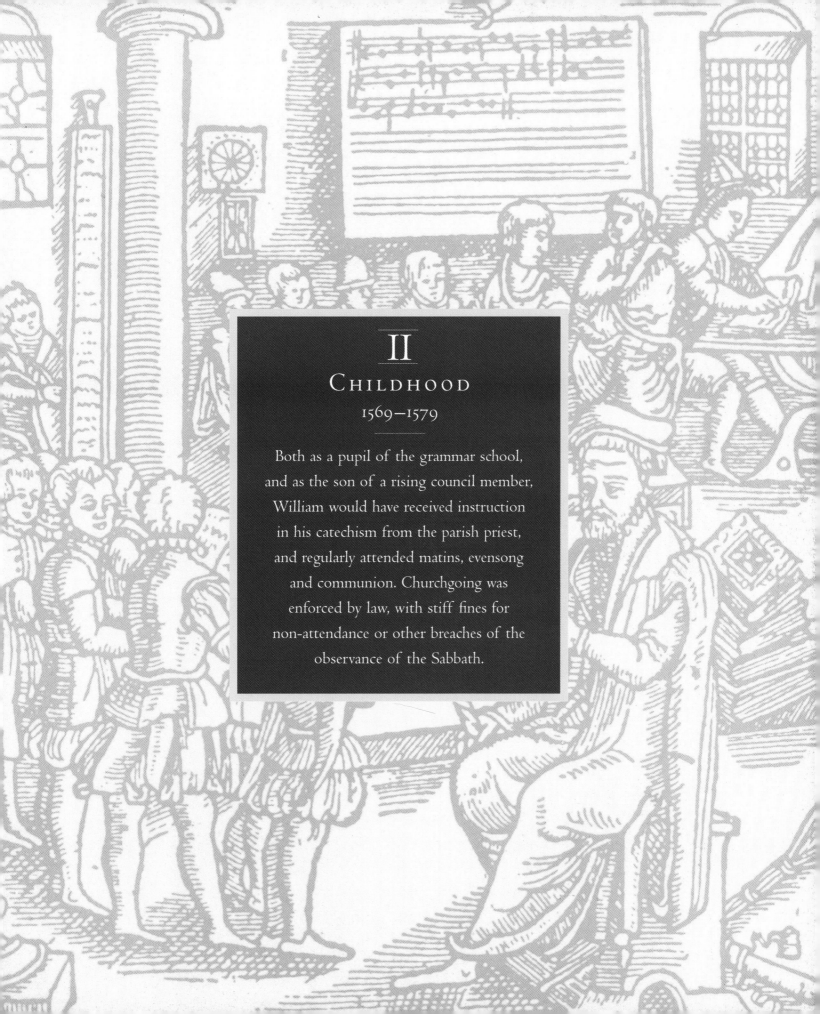

II
CHILDHOOD
1569–1579

Both as a pupil of the grammar school,
and as the son of a rising council member,
William would have received instruction
in his catechism from the parish priest,
and regularly attended matins, evensong
and communion. Churchgoing was
enforced by law, with stiff fines for
non-attendance or other breaches of the
observance of the Sabbath.

Ben Jonson famously said that his friend Will Shakespeare had 'small Latin and less Greek'. By the standards of our day, if not his own, Jonson was wrong about the Latin; but the myth persists that this particular poet, because he did not enjoy the university education of his literary contemporaries, 'wanted art' (Jonson again), that he was 'untaught, unpractised' (Dryden), that he was 'fancy's child' warbling his 'native woodnotes wild' (Milton).

There is no documentary evidence that Shakespeare attended Stratford's grammar school, the institution traditionally held to be his *alma mater*; the registers for the period, unsurprisingly, have not survived. But we have the word of his first biographer, Nicholas Rowe, that John Shakespeare installed his son 'for some time at a Free-School'; and only one such was available to the son of a civic eminence, the King's New School in Church Street, behind the Guild Chapel, only a few hundred yards' trudge from the family home in Henley Street. With the granting of its borough charter in 1553, amid the post-Reformation zeal for learning, Stratford had been as swift as other new townships to establish a school of the highest standards, run by a Master whose qualifications entitled him to a grace-and-favour house in the Guild precincts and the handsome stipend — more than Eton paid — of £20 a year.

School life in Shakespeare's time.
Unknown artist.

The all-male school's minimum age of entry was seven, but pupils as young as four or five began their studies at the adjacent 'petty school', under the wing of an '*abecedarius*' (or usher) appointed and paid by the Master. With the birth of the second Joan in the summer of 1569, amid the seemingly unstoppable upward mobility of John Shakespeare, we may thus envisage a reluctant five-year-old William buckling down to an arduous school routine at the behest of his impatient, ambi-

(PAGE 44)
SIXTEENTH-CENTURY
HORNBOOK READING AID.
(OPPOSITE)
PORTRAIT OF
SHAKESPEARE BY SOEST.

tious father. The long school day ran from 6 AM to 6 PM, beginning and ending with Protestant devotions, with only a two-hour lunch break at 11 otherwise interrupting fully ten hours of lessons every day, six days a week, every week of the year, except Holy Days — a very different thing from holidays, a concept alien to the Elizabethan schoolboy.

Once the alphabet was mastered, the Lord's Prayer was supplemented by *The ABC With the Catechism*, which added the catechism from the Book of Common Prayer and some mealtime graces. The third and most advanced of the standard textbooks was *The Primer and Catechism*, which featured the Calendar and Almanac, plus the seven penitential psalms and other religious texts. Thus were schoolboys scarce out of infancy weaned on *prosodia* (the 'pronouncing of letters, syllables, and words with the mouth') and *orthographia* (the 'writing of them with the hands'). Spelling, of course, was not yet considered a necessary skill; in the absence of any orthodoxy, spelling remained 'gloriously impressionistic', as Anthony Burgess noted with typical exuberance: 'To learne to wrytte doune Ingglisshe wourdes in Chaxper's daie was notte dificulte.'

These basic skills, plus perhaps the fundamentals of numeracy, would thus have been mastered by the time the seven-year-old Shakespeare graduated to the grammar school proper in 1571, the year his father was nominated Stratford's Chief Alderman. Now William's education would be in the hands of a succession of eminently qualified if pedantic pedagogues, by turns bookish and pious, all Oxford men of apparently unflinching rectitude. The pattern had been set in 1565, the year after Shakespeare's birth, by a devout friend of Vicar Bretchgirdle named John Brownsword, briefly followed in 1568 by a John Acton, a scholar of Brasenose College, Oxford. Another Oxford college, Corpus Christi, supplied his successor, the Lancastrian Walter Roche, who lasted only two years — probably those William spent at the petty school, hunched over his 'Absey' book and catechism — before departing to make more money as a lawyer.

CATECHISMVS
*paruus pueris primùm Latinè
qui ediſcatur, proponendus
in Scholis.*

LONDINI
Apud Iohannem Dayum Typographum. An. 1573.

Cum Priuilegio Regiæ Maieſtatis.

TITLE PAGE OF 'CATECHISMUS PARUUS PUERIS PRIMUM LATINE QUI EDISCATEUR', BY ALEXANDER NOWELL, 1573.

(OPPOSITE)
DR CAIUS, SIMPLE AND DAME QUICKLY, FROM 'THE MERRY WIVES OF WINDSOR', 1830. PAINTING BY ROBERT WALTER WEIR, 1803–89.

In 1571, the year of William's arrival in the senior school, Roche was succeeded as Master by Simon Hunt, who four years later matriculated at the Catholic University of Douai, became a Jesuit in 1578 and then penitentiary at St Peter's in Rome, where he died in 1585. Whatever impact he had on the young William, and whatever bonds he forged with his recusant father, Hunt moved on to self-imposed religious exile after just four years, having supervised the poet's education between the impressionable ages of seven and eleven. His successor turned out to be an equally significant childhood mentor, the self-made scholar-cleric Thomas Jenkins, who arrived as Master from Warwick grammar school. Son of an 'old servant' to Sir Thomas White, founder of St John's College, Oxford, Jenkins *fils* took his degree there, going on to become a Fellow of sufficient stature to be granted the lease of Chaucer's house at Woodstock.

Though Jenkins was a Londoner, his very name appears to have inspired the affectionate parody of a Welsh pedagogue in *The Merry Wives of Windsor*, in which Falstaff scorns Sir Hugh Evans for speaking 'Welsh flannel' and making 'fritters of English'. It can also be no coincidence that the name of Evans's pupil is William (one of only two characters in the canon to whom the playwright gave his own name).

Latin, *pace* Jonson, was the very core of the grammar school curriculum. Apart from Lily, with his declension and conjugations, and sample set texts for learning by rote, the seven-year-olds were force-fed such other Latin anthologies as Erasmus's *Cato* and the *Sententiae Pueriles* of Leonard Cullmann. They were introduced to Aesop's *Fables* via a Latin translation, and to the works of Terence and Plautus, scenes from whose comedies they regularly acted out. Armed with a dictionary, the boys of Stratford grammar school were already mastering the disciplines of written Latin by translating passages from the Geneva Bible, and spoken Latin via the colloquies of Corderius, Gallus or Vives, and the dialogues of Erasmus.

'THE SCHOOL MASTER' BY BOSSE 1602–76.

(OPPOSITE)
HERMIA AND LYSANDER,
FROM 'A MIDSUMMER
NIGHT'S DREAM'.
PAINTING BY
JOHN SIMMONS.

At the age of eleven, as schoolmaster Jenkins arrived in 1575, the young Shakespeare would have graduated to Cicero, Susenbrotus, Quintilian and Erasmus's *De Copia* as rhetoric and logic entered the senior school syllabus. These were the springboard for both written epistles and spoken orations. They were also the gateway to Virgil, Horace and Ovid, all of whom won a lasting place in Shakespeare's heart, above all Ovid's *Metamorphoses*, a prime source for so many poetic motifs. An affection for Juvenal is also heard in Hamlet's 'satirical rogue', though there are few such fond records of Persius, or the historians Sallust and Caesar, or Cicero's *De Officiis*, the standard school introduction to moral philosophy. 'Small Latin' to Ben Jonson, perhaps — but to one latter-day authority, Shakespeare would have left Stratford grammar school 'as well qualified in Latin as a modern classics graduate'.

'Less Greek' we may allow; Shakespeare's studies would have progressed barely, if at all, beyond some elementary dabbling in the baffling hieroglyphics of a Greek New Testament. As for lack of university 'polish': the universities of the day added no such gloss to a schoolboy's studies of classical literature or logic, rhetoric or moral philosophy, existing solely for vocational training in professions such as the law, medicine or divinity. The man of letters was not then regarded as having entered a profession.

Both as a pupil of the grammar school, and as the son of a rising council member, William would have received instruction in his catechism from the parish priest, and regularly attended matins, evensong and communion. Churchgoing was enforced by law, with stiff fines for non-attendance or other breaches of the observance of the Sabbath. But Shakespeare 'died a Papist,' testified Richard Davies, sometime chaplain of Corpus Christi College, Oxford, some seventy years after the poet's death. The most persuasive subsequent evidence also suggests that Shakespeare's father brought him up a secret Catholic, obliged to conform outwardly to Protestant orthodoxy, as was John Shakespeare himself as a member of the Stratford council. The young William would continue a furtive Papist for some years yet, as we shall see; but he was meanwhile steeped in Protestant orthodoxy throughout his schooldays, absorbing texts and tenets which echo through his work. Quotations from or references to no fewer than forty-two books of the Bible — eighteen each from

(PAGES 52–53)
FALSTAFF DISPELLED FROM FORD'S HOUSE, FROM 'THE MERRY WIVES OF WINDSOR'.
PAINTING BY JAMES DURNO, C.1745–95.

the Old and the New Testament, and six from the Apocrypha — have been identified throughout the plays and non-dramatic poems.

Just as there is no record of William Shakespeare's entry to Stratford grammar school, so there is no record of his leaving it. After a decade and more of intensive schooling, those few boys talented enough for university moved on around the age of fifteen, when the rest would have to square up to earning their living. In Shakespeare's case, there is good reason to believe that he left school even earlier.

William was only thirteen when his father's professional fortunes entered their sudden decline; the Stratford records show that the council meeting of 5 September 1576 was the last attended by the former bailiff, now Chief Alderman, for some years. Financial difficulties were not easy to conceal; a five-year-old suit for a debt of £30, pressed again in 1578 by Henry Higford of

THE GRAMMAR SCHOOL,
STRATFORD-UPON-AVON,
1907.
PAINTING BY
FRANCIS S. WALKER.

John Gilbert 1849

The Plays of
William Shakespeare,
1849.
Painting by
Sir John Gilbert
1817—97.

Solihull, is as conspicuous in the Stratford records as John Shakespeare's unexplained absence throughout 1557–78 from the deliberations of the council he had recently chaired.

That its members continued to hold him in affectionate regard, whatever the problems that kept him from their midst, is evidenced by several exemptions from the regular financial obligations incumbent on civic elders. The records for 29 January 1578 name John Shakespeare among several to be spared the statutory aldermanic payment towards the maintenance of three borough pikemen, two billmen and one archer. On 19 November he is again exempted from the weekly tax for the poor levied on all aldermen. Only the previous week, ominously, John and his wife are recorded to have sold 'seventy acres of land to Thomas Webbe and Humphrey Hooper'. This was part of Mary Arden's dowry. The family fortunes were indeed in trouble.

In such a crisis, what more natural than for proud John Shakespeare to remove his eldest son from school to make an early start at his father's side in the glover's shop and his mother's at the domestic hearth? Barely a century later, in 1701, Rowe suggested that 'the narrowness of his circumstances, and the want of his assistance at home, forced his father to withdraw him from thence' – to wit, the free-school. As early as 1577, the first year of John Shakespeare's reversals, John Aubrey has thirteen-year-old William working beside his father as 'a butcher'. And it is clear from repeated references throughout the canon that Shakespeare knew his butchery.

Over the ensuing four centuries, many other gossips and scholars have enlisted him in as many other trades besides, transfixed by the expertise of his many references to the law, medicine, the military, the navy, the court and the countryside – which can only have been deployed, it has been held, by a trained lawyer, doctor, soldier, sailor, nobleman, falconer, and/or scholar-gardener. For the plain fact is that, between his baptism in 1564, his marriage and the births of his children in 1583–85, a lawsuit in 1589 and the first mention of him as a London playwright in 1592, there is not one documented reference to William Shakespeare of Stratford-upon-Avon.

'Upon his leaving school,' according to Rowe, 'he seems to have given entirely into that way of living which his father proposed for him.' As an extra pair of hands in his father's shop, both out back and up front, his spare time spiced with some illicit butchery, he would soon have felt the need to spread his wings yet wider. The family's cashflow problems, though stabilised by selling off land and other assets, showed no signs of improvement. As anxious to broaden his own experience as to help his father, might Will have clerked for the Stratford lawyer handling John Shakespeare's ceaseless litigation? Might he have smuggled home shanks of meat for his mother from the animals whose hides furnished his father's wares? Might he even have tried to help his family through these straitened times, seeing it as his duty as the eldest son, with a little deer-poaching?

All these theories and more, many more, have been canvassed by four centuries of admirers, both amateur and professional, seeking to fill the troublesome gap between the end of Shakespeare's schooldays and his arrival in London. All we know for sure about the decade between his leaving school and arriving in London is that he married and fathered three children. The rest was, and will always remain, fertile territory for the literary gumshoe.

Shakespeare's most influential early biographer, Edmund Malone, suggested in 1790 that he had been employed 'while yet he remained at Stratford, in the office of some county attorney, who was at the same time a petty conveyancer, and perhaps also the Seneschal of some manor-court.' Malone was himself a barrister-turned-scholar. Legal clerking may seem unlikely at so young an age, dependent on no evidence beyond the remarkably wide range of legal terms expertly deployed throughout his work; with so much litigation dogging his father's life, and later his own, Shakespeare must have developed an intimate acquaintance with a veritable raft of lawyers, and absorbed the technical terms of their trade with the due relish of a born writer. He may, after his arrival in London, have spent some time in a lawyer's office, learning at least the art of the scrivener, or lawyer's copy-clerk.

NICHOLAS ROWE, 1674–1718, POET LAUREATE AND DRAMATIST. LINE ENGRAVING BY GEORGE VERTUE AFTER MONUMENT IN WESTMINSTER ABBEY BY JOHN M. RYSBRACK.

Far more convincing (not to say endearing) is the time-honoured thesis that the young Shakespeare fell foul of the local squire, Sir Thomas Lucy, for stealing his deer, and so was forced to flee Stratford. The tale took root as early as 1709, again with Nicholas Rowe, who has the newly married poet falling foul of Lucy for poaching in his park at Charlecote. The deer-stealing Shakespeare swiftly established a firm hold on literary imaginations, not least because the playwright devotes a hundred lines to the subject at the beginning of *The Merry Wives of Windsor*, in which Justice Shallow has been seen as a caricature of Sir Thomas Lucy.

Richard Davies, the seventeenth-century clergyman of Corpus Christi College, Oxford, embellished local lore with the intelligence that Shakespeare was 'much given to all unluckiness in stealing venison and rabbits, particularly from Sir — Lucy, who had him oft whipped and sometimes imprisoned and at last made him fly his native country.'

By 1763, the deer-poaching story had attained the respectability of a mention in the entry on Shakespeare in the *Biographica Britannica*, which spoke of continuing hostilities between the former bailiff's son and the indignant squire to the point where Lucy's anger drove Shakespeare 'to the extreme end of ruin, where he was forced to a very low degree of drudgery for a support.'

So how to solve the problem of Shakespeare's all but total disappearance from the public record between his schooldays and his unrecorded arrival in London? The year 1585 marks one of the few exceptions, as that in which his wife Anne gave birth to twins, whose baptism is recorded in the Stratford register on 2 February. It has become generally accepted as the starting-date for the so-called 'lost years' – when biographers can (and do) let their imaginations run riot. One twentieth-century scholar prefers to regard them as dating from his birth in 1564 – for, 'excepting the three dates 1582, 1583 and 1585 [his marriage and the baptisms of his three children], we have no certain knowledge of his activities or whereabouts during those 28 years'. If Shakespeare stayed at school until the age of fifteen or sixteen, when boys 'normally went to university', the 'lost' years would in fact seem best defined as the period from 1579 to 1592. But he may well have left school, as we have seen, even younger. So how (and where) did Shakespeare spend his teens?

(OPPOSITE)
EDMUND MALONE, 1778.
PAINTING BY
SIR JOSHUA REYNOLDS,
1723–92.

III

The 'lost' years
1579–1587

The plain fact is that, between
his baptism in 1564, his marriage
and the births of his children in
1583–85, a lawsuit in 1589
and the first mention of him as a
London playwright in 1592,
there is not one documented reference
to William Shakespeare of
Stratford-upon-Avon.

Dated 3 August 1581, and proved soon after his death the following month, the will of Alexander Hoghton Esq. of Lea, Lancashire, bequeathed to his half-brother Thomas all his musical instruments and his stock of 'play clothes', or costumes, 'if he be minded to keep & do keep players'. If Thomas were not so minded, the instruments and costumes were to pass to Alexander's neighbour and friend Sir Thomas Hesketh, kinsman of his second wife Elizabeth (*née* Hesketh), along with two players about whom the dying man added an earnest petition:

> *And I most heartily require the said Sir Thomas to be friendly unto Fulk Gyllome*
> *and William Shakeshafte now dwelling with me and either to take them unto his*
> *service or else to help them to some good master, as my trust is he will.*

William Shakeshafte is mentioned again later in the will, as one of eleven servants left an annuity of £2, on top of the year's wages bequeathed all Hoghton's staff. Four hundred years on, it now seems clear that this 'Shakeshafte' was in fact fifteen-year-old William Shakespeare — youthful tutor-turned-actor in a noble, wealthy and illicitly Catholic household in Lancashire.

'In his younger years,' testified John Aubrey, Shakespeare was 'a schoolmaster in the country'. Given the status of sixteenth-century surnames — infinitely flexible, as we have seen — there is scant cause for surprise in the change in name from Shakespeare to Shakeshafte. It can scarcely be called an alias, to cover a young Warwickshire Catholic's tentative tracks amid the network of informers then riddling boldly recusant Lancashire; but it perhaps had its uses as a variant. Shakespeare's grandfather Richard appears as Shakeschafte and Shakstaff as well as Shakspere in the Snitterfield records; in Lancashire, at the time, the familiar local variant was Shakeshafte — a natural enough name for an out-of-county man to assimilate.

Another such variant was 'Cotham' for Cottom. A Lancashire neighbour, friend and fellow recusant named John 'Cotham' was another beneficiary named in Alexander Hoghton's will; and that same John Cottom (in his own preferred spelling) just happened to be the teacher who took over as Master of Stratford grammar school in 1579. A Lancastrian, late of London, and a graduate of Brasenose College, Oxford, Cottom was Thomas Jenkins's personal

(PAGE 62)
QUEEN ELIZABETH I'S
PORTRAIT IN THE PLEA
ROLL OF THE COURT OF
THE QUEEN'S BENCH, 1581.
(OPPOSITE)
AUTOLYCUS IN THE
KITCHEN, FROM
'THE WINTER'S TALE'.
PAINTING BY
HARRY ROBERT
MILEHAM, 1873–1957.

choice as his successor. Apart from the London-born Welshman Jenkins, every one of the five Masters of the Stratford school from 1569 to 1624 happened to be a Lancashire man, all Catholics.

It would thus seem no coincidence that Jenkins's predecessor, that other Lancastrian Simon Hunt, took himself off to Douai University before turning Jesuit and devoting himself to Rome. Among Douai's wealthy benefactors was Thomas Hoghton, Alexander's older brother, whose estate constituted the contents of the will in which Shakeshafte was remembered. The son of Sir Richard de Hoghton (1498–1559), Thomas was a recusant so unrepentant, and indeed so prominent, as to be forced to opt for permanent exile from England in 1569, dying eleven years later in Liége.

The sixteenth-century Hoghtons have been described as 'one of the premier families of Lancashire', descended directly from one of William the Conqueror's companions, and through the female line from the legendary Lady Godiva of Coventry, wife of Leofric, Earl of Mercia. While still in Lancashire, in charge of the family fortunes, Thomas had rebuilt the family seat, Hoghton Tower, on a ridge six miles south-east of Preston – where still it stands, housing his descendants.

Although inevitably neglected after Thomas's departure in 1569, the Hoghton estate remained substantial at the time of his death in 1580. As a priest his son was debarred from succeeding, so it passed to his younger brother Alexander, who died childless the following year. Now the estate passed to his half-brother, another Thomas, who faithfully carried out Alexander's instructions. The name of Fulke Gyllome, so closely linked with Shakeshafte's in the Hoghton will, appears twice in subsequent Hesketh records, as witness to legal documents in 1591 and 1608.

So Thomas Hoghton was not, it seems, minded to keep players, with or without their instruments and costumes – and they did indeed pass, as Alexander had wished, to his noble and even wealthier friend Hesketh. Even the musical instruments are mentioned in subsequent Hesketh inventories. Both they and the two Hoghton players, Gyllome and Shakeshafte, would have been pressed into service when plays were laid on for significant visitors.

Lancashire was a hotbed of recusancy at a time when Elizabeth's govern-

(OPPOSITE)
ORSINO AND VIOLA, FROM
'TWELFTH NIGHT'.
PAINTING BY FREDERICK
RICHARD PICKERSGILL,
1820–1900.

ment was intensifying its periodic purges on Roman Catholics, many of whom were at the least fined or imprisoned, at worst tortured and publicly executed. New legislation 'to retain the Queen's Majesty's subjects in due obedience' received the royal assent on 18 March 1581, only months before Alexander made his will. Hoghton Tower was one of many safe havens for papists in Lancashire under constant surveillance by both covert informers and authorised agents of the Privy Council, in whose name frequent raids were mounted. Many leading Lancashire families, including the Hoghtons, made a public show of 'conforming' while secretly harbouring priests in their households.

One such was Thomas Cottom, younger brother of the Stratford schoolmaster John, a friend and associate of the Jesuit Edmund Campion, who visited the Hoghton household 'between Easter and Whitsuntide' 1581. Campion was arrested that July, and arraigned on 12 November 1581, two days before Cottom (who had been arrested on his return to England from Italy in June 1580). Among the evidence against Campion was that he had been staying with leading Catholic families in Lancashire, whose houses had been searched by order of the Privy Council — 'especially,' according to its records, 'the house of Richard Hoghton', in whose safekeeping he had left his books. After torture on the rack, Cottom and Campion were publicly executed as traitors — or Roman Catholic martyrs — on 1 December 1581 and 13 May 1582 respectively.

Campion was the source of the copy of the testament lurking in the Shakespeare home in Stratford, if not yet hidden in the roof. Can it be mere coincidence that John Cottom resigned his Stratford post in 1581, while his brother languished in the Marshalsea, and returned to Lancashire, to his father's estate at Tarnacre, hard by the Hoghton property of Alston Hall, ten miles from the family seat at Lea? Between

PRINT DEPICTING THE PERSECUTION OF ENGLISH CATHOLICS. FROM 'THEATRUM CRUDELITATUM HAERETICORUM NOSTRI TEMPORIS', 1587.

Persecutiones aduersus Catholicos à Protestantibus Caluinistis excitæ in Anglia.

Sanguinis effusi firmamus pignore Christi
Maiorumá, fidem, magni fundamina Petri,
Et tantum Latijs apicem veneramur in oris.
At gregis electi custodia non cadet vnquam
In caput, ô Regina, tuum, regésque profanos,
Et minus in vilem fidei mysteria sexum.

L 2   MARIA

his return and his death in 1616, Cottom inherited his father's property and openly acknowledged his Catholicism. Less belligerent than his martyred brother, he was regarded by the authorities as less dangerous; faced with recusant fines rather than arrest and torture, he avoided his brother's grim fate by paying up.

At the time of John Cottom's arrival in Stratford in 1579, Shakespeare was fifteen years old and his father's affairs in ever more rapid decline. This was an '*annus horribilis*' for the Shakespeare family, who that April buried another child, William's eight-year-old sister Anne. The previous month, John Shakespeare's levy of 3s 4d for arms had gone 'unpaid and unaccounted for'; by Easter he was raising £40 by the drastic move of mortgaging what was left of his wife's dowry, Asbies, comprising a house and sixty acres in Wilmcote, to his brother-in-law Edmund Lambert, husband of Mary's sister Joan.

P, THOMAS CATTAMVS ANGL' *Londini pro fide Cat.ª suspensus gla dioque sectus .9,Iul. 1582.*

UNATTRIBUTED ENGRAVING OF
THOMAS COTTOM.

The wealthy Lambert lived fifteen miles south of Stratford in the small village of Barton on the Heath, apparently as familiar to the young William as the inn at Wilmcote, or Wincot, half-way between the two, mentioned in the Induction to *The Taming of the Shrew*. The previous autumn, Lambert had also been named in the will of Roger Sadler, a baker of Stratford High Street, as surety for '£5, the debt of Mr John Shakspere'. Clearly the glover was growing deep in debt to his brother-in-law. When the £40 borrowed in 1579 fell due the following year, John was unable to repay it; so Lambert held on to the estate, of which he was still in possession when he died seven years later. There followed protracted litigation in the High Court as John Shakespeare tried to recover the property from Lambert's son and heir, his nephew John, who counter-sued on the grounds that further debts were due.

Fred. Bodtuls junior Sculp:

P. EDMONDVS CAMPIANVS, ROBERTVS S'HERWINVS, ende ALEXANDER BRIANTVS van de
Societeijt IESV worden te Londen voor het gheloof ghehanghen ende ghevierendeelt.

The Asbies estate would never be recovered by the Shakespeares. But worse was to follow in October 1579, when John was forced to sell off more of his children's potential inheritance; John and Mary Shakespeare's joint interest in two 'messuages' at Snitterfield — her one-ninth share of her father's property, comprising two houses and 100 acres of land — was sold to another relative, Robert Webbe, for a mere £4. 'Yeoman' John Shakespeare and his wife both made their usual marks by way of signing the deed of sale.

Throughout 1579 Stratford's former bailiff was still absent from all its recorded council meetings. With another child on the way — a third son, Edmund, named after their obliging relative Lambert, would be born the following April — William had become simply another mouth to feed. It was time for him to set about earning his own living. That same year, the record shows, his schoolfriend Richard Field, son of the Stratford tanner Henry Field, began a seven-year apprenticeship to a London printer. 'Being taken from school by their parents,' according to Sir Thomas Elyot's 1531 manual on the education of the governing classes, the 'aptest and most proper scholars . . . either be brought to court, and made lackeys or pages, or else are bounden prentices.'

Given a secret Catholic bond between the Shakespeare family and the newly arrived schoolmaster John Cottom, what could be more natural than accepting his help in sending William to an enviable job — perhaps even to train secretly as a seminarist — a hundred miles away in Lancashire? Alexander Hoghton was landlord to Cottom's father at Tarnacre. His own secret links with the other Cottom son, coupled with the benevolence evident in his will, would have seen Hoghton readily agree to take in one of Stratford grammar school's most brilliant recent pupils — a kindred spirit in more ways than one — as tutor to his own children, or those of his staff, while pursuing his religious instruction.

Shakespeare would have been a Hoghton hireling at least a year, more like two, by the time he moved on to Hesketh's employ ten miles south-east at Rufford Old Hall in the latter part of 1581. Seventeen and eager to please, Shakespeare had clearly impressed his first employer more as a player than a potential priest. Now he would have a real chance to shine onstage, as the grander Hesketh household regularly received visiting troupes of actors — including such leading groups as the Earl of Derby's Players, later those of his son and heir Ferdinando, Lord Strange, and eventually a source of recruitment for the Lord Chamberlain's Men.

That same year, 1581, saw Sir Thomas Hesketh's arrest as 'a disaffected Papist'. Contemporary documents suggest that he was soon released, on an undertaking to 'reform' his household by way of suppressing Catholic worship. Although briefly arrested again three years later, Hesketh seems otherwise to have managed to satisfy the authorities that Rufford Old Hall was no longer a hotbed of Papist sedition — even though, intriguingly, repairs to the Great Hall uncovered a secret chamber or 'priest's hole' in the west gable as recently as 1939.

Forty-six feet long, twenty-two feet wide and eighteen feet high, that same Great Hall would have been the site of performances by Sir Thomas Hesketh's *ad hoc* group of resident players, and those of visiting troupes such as those of his friend Henry Stanley, Earl of Derby. The close connection between the noble houses of Hesketh and Stanley/Derby is amply documented, with regular visits between them recorded throughout this period in the *Derby Household Book*.

It seems unlikely that William stayed long in the employ, however enlightened, of Sir Thomas Hesketh — but long enough to gain a glimpse of life under Lord Derby, whose professional troupe of actors toured the country while Hesketh merely laid on occasional entertainments provided by members of his staff, who doubled as tutors and musicians more than players. Nor was the Hesketh household as openly Catholic as Hoghton's. Shakespeare, or Shakeshafte, would soon have felt under-employed, perhaps even out of place, at Rufford Old Hall. Might his new patron Hesketh, by all accounts a benevolent employer, have heeded the words of his late friend Alexander Hoghton, and seen it as his duty to 'help' this talented young man to some other 'good master'? If so, who more obvious — and close to hand — than his friend Lord Derby, a close friend of the Queen with his own troupe of players to absorb the ambitious and talented kindred spirit from Stratford.

But Shakespeare could not have gone straight to London with the Earl of Derby's Players in 1581, as has been suggested. However sketchy our knowledge

HENRY STANLEY,
4TH EARL OF DERBY.
PAINTING BY
ISAAC OLIVER,
C.1565–1617.

of Shakespeare's late teens, we know one thing for sure. By the following summer, certainly by August 1582, he was back home in Stratford-upon-Avon.

The fortunes of Shakespeare's father had not improved during William's absence. In 1580 John had been fined £20 for his failure to appear in the Court of the Queen's Bench with a guarantee to keep the Queen's peace, and a further £20 by the same court as a result of his surety on the same grounds on behalf of a Nottingham hatmaker, John Audeley. No record survives to show that he actually paid these fines; but between them, they would have wiped out the £40 mortgage borrowed from his brother-in-law, Lambert. John Shakespeare seemed to have been paying the price for his somewhat indiscriminate choice of friends in more prosperous times, when he appears to have bailed out all and sundry; now he forfeited his bond of £10 of a debt of £22 incurred by his wayward brother Henry, and the bail he had stood for Michael Price, the skul-duggerous Stratford tinker. Only by begging his friend Alderman Hill to stand bail on his own behalf did John avoid the ultimate indignity of incarceration.

The records for 1581 show that John Shakespeare still failed to attend a single council meeting, though the year appears mercifully free of further financial transactions. We can only assume that John and Mary Shakespeare were pleased to see their eldest son returned from his lengthy sojourn up north, if less than ecstatic about his excited talk of a life in the theatre. John had troubles of his own that summer, falling out seriously enough with four old friends — William Russell, Thomas Logginge, Robert Young and the butcher Ralph Cawdrey, then bailiff — to petition for sureties of the peace against them 'for fear of death and mutilation of his limbs'. The last thing John needed was the trouble young William was about to cause.

Sometime that August, after wandering the mile or so west down the rural footpath to the tiny village of Shottery, the worldly eighteen-year-old committed an indiscretion which would profoundly affect the rest of his life. It is hard to believe that this ambitious young dreamer, already aware there was a world elsewhere, way beyond rural Warwickshire, was so enamoured of a homely wench eight years his senior — the same age as Juliet's mother, who is already impatient for grandchildren — as to want to marry her. Or did the local farmer's twenty-six-year-old daughter, only a month after her father's death, set out to catch herself a much younger husband by seducing him? Either way, the autumn of 1582 saw Anne Hathaway telling her late father's friends that she was pregnant by young Will Shakespeare, teenage son of the Stratford alderman.

There is no extant record of Anne Hathaway's birth or christening, as she was born before baptismal registers commenced in 1558. The brass plate on her tomb in Stratford's Holy Trinity church testifies that she 'departed this life' on 6 August 1623, 'being of the age of 67 years'. So she would have been born in 1556, eight years before her future husband. By her mid-twenties, life at Hewland's farm cannot have been easy for Anne – a displaced person since her father's death, living with a stepmother and three stepbrothers, probably as eager to marry her off as was she herself to escape them.

Was Shakespeare trapped into a reluctant marriage by a desperate woman eight years his senior, scared of being left on the shelf in a home no longer her own? Or was this a genuine love-match? Whatever Will's feelings, two of the late Farmer Hathaway's close friends, Fulke Sandells and John Richardson, came knocking on the door of the Shakespeare home in Henley Street that autumn, demanding that the son of the house do the right thing by their deceased friend's pregnant daughter.

Or so we may surmise. Sandells was named in Richard Hathaway's will as one of his two trustees, or executors; Richardson made his mark as a witness. The distinct impression given by the bare documentation of subsequent events is that these two worthies strong-armed young William over to the consistory court at Worcester, some twenty miles from Stratford, before he could flee his obligations. It has even been suggested that Sandells and Richardson obtained the licence on their own initiative, with or without the knowledge of Shakespeare's father, to ensure that the father of Anne Hathaway's future child duly became her husband. If so, they were willing to pledge the huge sum of £40 between them to guarantee the marriage, which was duly authorised in a document dated 28 November 1582, authorising the union (after only one reading of the banns) between 'William Shagspere' and 'Anne Hathwey of Stratford in the diocese of Worcester, maiden'. It was also, presumably, the loyal Sandells and Richardson who testified to Anne's dubious standing as a

(OPPOSITE)
HAMLET AND THE
GRAVE DIGGER, 1883.
PAINTING BY
PASCAL DAGNAN-
BOUVERET,
1852–1929.

'maiden'; the clergy of the day were broad-minded enough to be prepared to substitute 'single-woman' where, as in this case, appropriate.

Anne Hathaway's name may now echo through literary history, not least as attached to the cottage still visited today by 200,000 tourists a year, but she was actually born with the name of Agnes. That much is clear from her father's will, made the previous summer, in which he details bequests for his four sons and three daughters, including ten marks to be paid to his daughter Agnes on her wedding day. It seems that the names Agnes and Anne, like Shaxpere and Shakespeare, were virtually interchangeable.

Her role in Shakespeare's life is further complicated by another entry in the Worcester diocesan records, dated the previous day, 27 November 1582, granting a licence for William Shaxpere of Stratford to marry one 'Anne Whateley of Temple Grafton'. This Anne Whateley appears in no other contemporary document yet discovered, certainly none relating to our poet. Who could she have been? The dull but probable answer is that she is the Elizabethan equivalent of a typing error. The same Worcester clerk, it has been observed, was slapdash enough to write 'Baker' for 'Barbar', 'Darby' for 'Bradeley', and 'Edgcock' for 'Elcock'. 'Whateley' for 'Hathaway' is a transfor-

mation of quite a different order; but a likely explanation lies close at hand. On the day the Hathaway licence was issued, the Worcester court dealt with no fewer than forty cases, including that of the vicar of Crowle, one William Whateley, pursuing non-payment of tithes from Arnold Leight. This Whateley appears to have been a regular litigant, his name occurring frequently in the court records for 1582–83. For a clerk in a hurry to substitute his name for that of Wm Shaxpere's intended seems understandable.

On 26 May 1583, Trinity Sunday, the Reverend Henry Heicroft christened the child of the six-months-married William and Anne Shakespeare with the uncommon and resoundingly Puritan name of Susanna. Was it a consciously ironical choice? Or were Shakespeare's religious beliefs already on the wane?

Now nineteen, but yet to find regular employment, he would have taken his bride to live with his parents at the capacious, double-fronted family home in Henley Street. They could not afford a home of their own; in cashflow terms Anne's dowry was small, only £6 13s 4d – 'to be paid unto her,' according to the terms of her father's will, 'at the day of her marriage'. Her mother-in-law would no doubt have delighted in having her first grandchild under her own roof, and enjoyed sharing the considerable burden of childcare; William's brother Edmund was, after all, only two years older than his newborn niece; Gilbert, Joan and Richard were respectively sixteen, thirteen and eight. Would an aspirant young poet, however, have relished life in such a household as much as his wife and mother?

Within two years, Anne would bear him two more children, twins named Hamnet and Judith after their friends Judith and Hamnet Sadler, who lived next to the Corn Market, on the corner of High Street and Sheep Street; when the Sadlers produced their own son thirteen years later, they returned the compliment by christening him William. The twins were christened on 2 February 1585 by Heicroft's successor as vicar of Stratford, Richard Barton of Coventry – a 'learned, zealous and godly' minister, by one Puritan report. Approaching his twenty-first birthday, Shakespeare was still living at home with his parents. Already he had enjoyed a taste of the world beyond Stratford; already he would have listened in local taverns to travellers' tales about London and its cosmopolitan excitements.

(OPPOSITE)
PERDITA SURROUNDED
BY THE THREE FURIES,
ARIEL IN THE
BACKGROUND, FROM 'THE
WINTER'S TALE', 1785.
PAINTING BY JOHANN
HEINRICH FÜSSLI,
1741–1825.

KATE,
FROM 'TAMING OF
THE SHREW'.
PAINTING BY THOMAS
FRANCIS DICKSEE,
1819–95.

So when did Shakespeare finally leave Stratford for London, to seek his fortune as an actor-playwright? He may have left us a clue in the words of a wise old Shepherd in one of his last plays, *The Winter's Tale*:

> *I would there were no age between ten and three-and-twenty, or that youth would sleep out the rest: for there is nothing in between but getting wenches with child, wronging the ancientry, stealing, fighting.*

As the mature Shakespeare looks back over his life, which had by this stage included its share of the youthful adventures he catalogues, twenty-three seems a very specific age to choose. Uniquely, the number crops up twice more in the same play. In 1587, the year Shakespeare turned twenty-three, Stratford enjoyed a visit from the leading theatrical troupe of the moment – the Queen's Men, handpicked for Elizabeth four years before by the Master of the Revels, clad in royal scarlet, and starring Richard Tarleton, the leading clown of his day (and forerunner of Yorick).

Before reaching Stratford, the Queen's Men played Abingdon, where the clamour to see them provoked a small riot; and Thame, where their performance on 13 June was followed by an incident which appears to have altered Shakespeare's life. That night, between the hours of 9 and 10 PM, a drunken quarrel broke out between two of the players, John Towne of Shoreditch and William Knell. In a close known as White Hound, Knell drew his sword and came at Towne, who found himself cornered. Drawing his own weapon, he plunged it into the neck of the advancing Knell, who died on the spot within half an hour. Pleading self-defence, Towne was spared by the local coroner and eventually pardoned by the Queen herself.

Within a year Knell's widow was remarried – to another actor, John Heminges, who would become a close friend of Shakespeare, a beneficiary of his will, and one of the editors of the indispensable First Folio of his collected plays. At the time, it was probably within a few days that the Queen's Men arrived in Stratford – one player short. Did they find a willing volunteer in twenty-three-year-old William Shakespeare, indigent father-of-three, son of a troubled father, anxious for steady work and prepared to travel? Was it with the Queen's Men, as their newest and most junior recruit, that the future playwright first found his way to London?

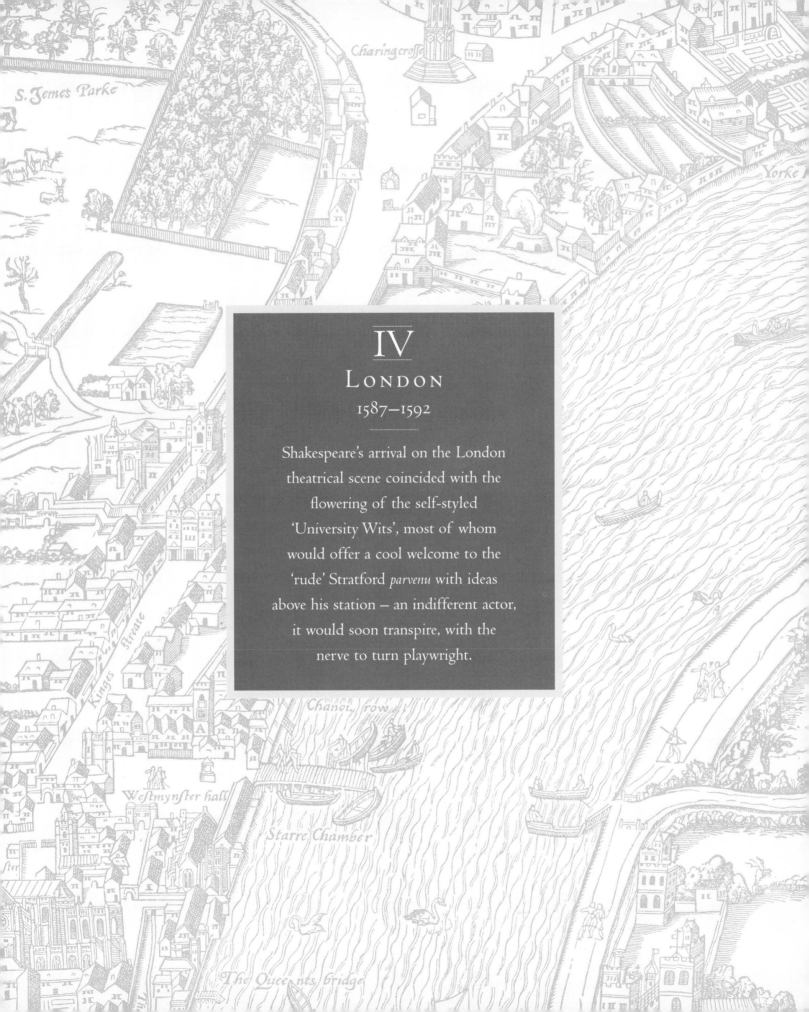

IV

LONDON

1587–1592

Shakespeare's arrival on the London
theatrical scene coincided with the
flowering of the self-styled
'University Wits', most of whom
would offer a cool welcome to the
'rude' Stratford *parvenu* with ideas
above his station — an indifferent actor,
it would soon transpire, with the
nerve to turn playwright.

Aldgate to the east; Bishopsgate, Moorgate, Cripplegate and Aldersgate to the north; Newgate and Ludgate to the west: today only the names survive of the seven entrances to the Elizabethan city of London through the two-mile wall enclosing it on three sides, the fourth consisting of the wharves and warehouses of the thriving port along the sprawling River Thames. Compared with the sweetly flowing waters of the rural Avon, those of the Thames were pestilentially filthy, thick with excrement and carrion, nourishing rats and breeding disease.

Upon its silvery surface, undeterred, a bustling water-traffic vied for space with elegant, three-masted schooners disgorging their cargo for sale at Billingsgate and other markets. With London Bridge the only way to cross the river by foot — and that crowded by the shops and dwellings of prosperous merchants, every inch of its eight hundred feet a vision of Shylock's Rialto — water-taxis plied a busy trade. With cries of 'Eastward Ho!' or 'Westward Ho!' they picked their way between the splendid private barges of the wealthy, not least the Queen herself, who liked to spend the occasional festive evening leading a flotilla of small craft up and down the river amid music and fire-works.

SOUTH-WEST VIEW OF OLD ST PAULS, LONDON, 1561.
UNKNOWN ARTIST.

To the west, then as now, the London skyline was dominated by St Paul's, even pre-Wren one of England's largest and most splendid cathedrals, yet still as much a place of commerce as of worship. To the east lay the rather more secular, brooding presence of the Tower of London, whose dark and blood-stained mysteries haunt so many of his plays, as indeed the lives of his friends and contemporaries. Beyond lay open countryside — apart from the fledgling hamlet of Islington, first stop on the Roman road to St Albans, past the lush forests of Hampstead hills. Beyond the city limits, to the west and south, lay the rural villages of St Pancras and Charing Cross.

Within the city walls, crammed into a maze of passages and alleyways, lived a population fast approaching 200,000 — almost a tenth of all England. Here London life was at its most cosmopolitan, coloured by countless refugees

(PAGE 86)
WILLIAM HERBERT, 3RD
EARL OF PEMBROKE.
UNKNOWN ARTIST.
(OPPOSITE)
MARY, QUEEN OF SCOTS.
UNKNOWN ARTIST.

from religious persecution all over Europe. Most lived in squalid, rubbish-strewn slums, their streets awash with excrement and urine, a rich breeding-ground for the black rat and its deadly parasite, the flea that carried and transmitted the bubonic plague. With no effective sewage system, it was said that London could be smelled twenty miles away.

The regular outbreaks of plague in the capital would play as significant a role in Shakespeare's work as the other events crowding his life and Catholic times — most recently the execution of Mary, Queen of Scots, in February 1587, shortly before his arrival in a capital readying itself for war with Spain.

Within a year came the defeat of Philip's Armada, inspired by the Queen's memorable lines at Tilbury — worthy of Shakespeare's *Henry V* at Agincourt — that within 'the body of a weak and feeble woman' lay 'the heart and stomach of a king, and a king of England too.' It was a high time to be English, an inspirational time to be a writer arriving at the heart of an unfolding political drama.

With Catholic purges renewed, and more Jesuit equivocators executed, Shakespeare seems wisely to have kept his own counsel about his religion — if, indeed, it still meant

EXECUTION OF MARY, QUEEN OF SCOTS, C.1608.
WATERCOLOUR BY AN UNKNOWN DUTCH ARTIST.

much to him. As an 'uneducated' country boy, newly arrived in a city full of smart, self-satisfied university graduates, he would now have to learn to pick his way through other forms of prejudice and intrigue. His arrival on the London theatrical scene coincided with the flowering of the self-styled 'University Wits', most of whom would offer a cool welcome to the 'rude' Stratford *parvenu* with ideas above his station — an indifferent actor, it would soon transpire, with the nerve to turn playwright.

OPHELIA, FROM 'HAMLET', 1867. PAINTING BY CARL FRIEDRICH WILHELM TRAUTSCHOLD, 1815–77.

Blessed be the great God of my salvation

Hollanders

2.KINGS.6.16.

Omnes effecti Deus, hic vultu&c. deher.
Et Committit Venturi ad Christum venit

SING VNTO THE LORD A NEW SONG FOR HE HATH DONE MARVELOVS THINGES HIS RIGHT HAND AND HIS HOLY ARME HATH
GOTTEN HIM TH. VICTORY AND ALL THE ENDS OF TH. EARTH HAVE SEENE THE SALVATION OF OVR GOD. Selah

How greate o Lord, shall the
Kinge reioyse in thy saluation

Often Flaming,
Neuer Confumin

In memory of the
Gunpowder Treason Plot 1605

Primus inter pares – before Shakespeare's arrival – was Christopher ('Kit') Marlowe, born the same year as the Stratford man, the son of a Canterbury shoemaker who had won himself a place at Corpus Christi College, Cambridge. Already, as Shakespeare arrived in London, Marlowe's *Tamburlaine* was holding the stage; over the next five years, before his violent and premature death in 1593, Marlowe would follow up with *Dr Faustus*, *The Jew of Malta* and *Edward II*.

The Tragicall Historie of the Life and Death of Doctor Faustus.

With new Additions.

Written by CH. MAR.

Printed at London for *Iohn Wright*, and are to be fold at his fhop without Newgate. 1631.

TITLE PAGE OF MARLOWE'S 'TRAGICALL HISTORIE OF THE LIFE AND DEATH OF DOCTOR FAUSTUS', 1631.

Jockeying for equal billing were such lesser talents as Robert Greene, Thomas Nashe, George Peele, Thomas Lodge, John Lyly – young Oxbridge graduates all, often joining forces as much as blazing their own trails in churning out box-office fodder as fast as the acting troupes could stage it. Rivals on whom they looked down, like Shakespeare's fellow grammar-school boy Thomas Kyd, whose *Spanish Tragedy* would prove such a success, were sneered at in ruthless satires. Mocking an early play by an anonymous hand (or hands), Lodge wrote in his *Wit's Miserie* about a devil 'as pale as the vizard of the ghost who cried so miserably at the Theatre, like an oyster-wife, *Hamlet, revenge!*' In 1588, within a year of Shakespeare's arrival in London, Nashe launched an attack on certain unnamed translators and writers as having only 'a little country grammar knowledge'. Rather more specific was the object of Peele's angst in his *Edward I*, written the following year:

> Shake thy speres, in honour of his name
> Under whose royalty thou wearst the same.

Marlowe was a case apart; an elegant and civilised talent, admired, aped and mourned by Shakespeare, he was largely diverted from the theatrical in-fighting by his work as a spy in the service of the Queen's elder statesman, Sir Francis Walsingham. Shakespeare probably knew Marlowe, and enjoyed his lively company – we cannot, with any confidence, assume much more – and he would pay him posthumous homage as the dead shepherd in *As You Like It*,

(PAGES 92–93) DIPTYCH DEPICTING THE ARRIVAL OF QUEEN ELIZABETH I AT TILBURY, THE DEFEAT OF THE SPANISH ARMADA AND THE GUNPOWDER PLOT. (OPPOSITE) SIR FRANCIS WALSINGHAM. PAINTING BY JOHN DE CRITZ, THE ELDER, C.1555–1641.

putting a line from Marlowe's *Hero and Leander* in the mouth of the shepherdess Phebe:

Dead shepherd, now I find thy saw of might

'Who ever lov'd that lov'd not at first sight?'

The rest of the 'University Wits' preened themselves in ornate, erudite poetry and polemical pamphlets, stooping to the writing of plays merely as a handy new way, if somewhat beneath their dignity, of making money.

It was barely a decade before Shakespeare's arrival in London, in 1576, that the same James Burbage who had passed through Stratford as a player – like Snug, he was a joiner-turned-actor – had the bright idea that 'continual great profit' might accrue from the erection of a building designed purely for the presentation of plays.

A 'playhouse' was a wholly original notion; hitherto, the dramatic art had flourished in the courtyards of inns such as Burbage's own Red Lion, built in 1567 by his brother-in-law John Brayne. With a hefty loan from Brayne, a prosperous grocer, Burbage took a twenty-one-year lease on a patch of waste land in Shoreditch, beside the Finsbury Fields at Holywell, only half a mile outside the Bishopsgate entrance to the city. Near what is today Liverpool Street Station, on a derelict site rank with weeds, bones and all manner of detritus, he duly constructed the world's first custom-built playhouse, which he proudly christened the Theatre (from the Greek *theatron*).

Like the imitators it soon spawned, Burbage's Theatre was modelled on the design of the inn-yards which had hitherto served the turns of theatrical troupes so well: a circular auditorium, with tiered galleries offering better, drier and more expensive seats for the gentry, and food and drink available for the 'groundlings' who paid a penny each to stand beneath the elements, crowding forward towards an elevated, rectangular stage,

TITLE PAGE OF KYD'S 'SPANISH TRAGEDIE', 1615.

The Spanish Tragedie:

OR,

Hieronimo is mad againe.

Containing the lamentable end of *Don Horatio*, and *Belimperia*; with the pittifull death of *Hieronimo*.

Newly corrected, amended, and enlarged with new Additions of the *Painters* part, and others, as it hath of late been diuers times acted.

LONDON,
Printed by W. White, for I. White and T. Langley, and are to be sold at their Shop ouer against the Sarazens head without New-gate. 1615.

(PAGES 96–97)
THE SPANISH ARMADA IN
THE STRAITS OF DOVER.
BY AN UNKNOWN FLEMISH
ARTIST.

flanked by two columns supporting a protective canopy known as 'the heavens'. On each side of the stage was a door for exits and entrances, at the back a curtained recess suitable for more intimate scenes.

This was the basic design that, for most of Shakespeare's working life, shaped his drama, large-scale or small. Above the 'heavens' was a thatched loft or 'attic' with openings available for use as upstairs windows, as in Juliet's balcony scene; later, this housed the equipment for 'flying'

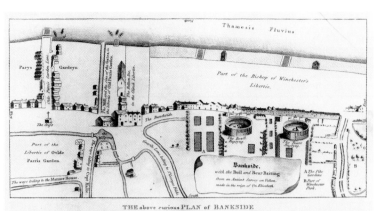

PLAN OF BANKSIDE SHOWING ARENAS FOR
BULL AND BEAR BAITING, C.1570.

effects, such as the descent of Jupiter in *Cymbeline*. From its roof flew a flag bearing the theatre company's symbol, raised as an advertisement before and during a performance, whose start was signalled by a liveried trumpeter. Below the stage, via a trap-door, was a storage area known as 'hell', convenient for such occasional use as the 'cellarage' haunted by the Ghost of Hamlet's Father. Behind the entire edifice, invisible to the audience, was the tiring-house (or dressing-room), a cramped space for actors to change their costumes and properties to be stored. Scenery, apart from the occasional bench, was minimal; the painting of scenes was in those days the job of the playwright. Soon Burbage's prototype Theatre had naturally lent its name to the type of building it fostered, and eventually to the activity it housed.

Within months of the Theatre's opening, early in 1577, another playhouse arose just two hundred yards to the south, also on Holywell Lane, in a dingy alley called Curtain Close. The Curtain was built not by a player, but a gentleman of means named Henry Laneman. For all Laneman's respectability, the sudden emergence of two such places of entertainment moved London churchmen to splutters of indignation. 'Behold these sumptuous houses, a continual monument of London's prodigality and folly!' preached Thomas White, vicar of St Dunstan's-in-the-West, at Paul's Cross in November 1577.

'It is an evident token of a wicked time,' thundered William Harrison, canon of Windsor, 'when players wax so rich that they can build such houses.'

For whatever reason – perhaps because it was run by actors, with a keener sense of what the public wanted – Burbage's Theatre fared better than Laneman's Curtain, which was forced by 1579 to resort to staging bouts of fencing. By 1585 the two impresarios had agreed to pool their resources, and the Curtain became an 'easer', or annexe, to the Theatre. By then, however, the centre of theatrical gravity was already shifting south of the river, to the Paris (short for 'Paradise') Garden – an unruly area around Bankside, where a large open meadow was the setting for running and wrestling, bowling and archery alongside the bearpits and brothels lining the riverbank. Here, in 1587, on the site of a former rose-garden, an entrepreneur named Philip Henslowe built a third playhouse, the Rose, in partnership with a wealthy grocer, John Cholmley. Also a pawnbroker and brothel-keeper, Henslowe went on to become the great theatrical impresario of his day. His account-books, an engagingly candid log of his expenditure and box-office receipts, are an invaluable source of information about the dates and venues of numerous plays by Shakespeare and others.

Soon would follow one more playhouse, the Swan, opened in 1596, also on the river's edge at the western end of Bankside, capable of holding all of 3,000 paying customers. At the time of Shakespeare's arrival in London, however, there were just the three more or less thriving theatres, all standing symbolically outside the city boundaries in areas aptly known as 'liberties'. Completed in February 1592 at a total cost of £100, the Rose became the home of Lord Strange's Men, now merged with the Admiral's Men, and led by the most admired actor of the day, Edward ('Ned') Alleyn. Shakespeare may already have met Alleyn on his visits to Stratford, perhaps earlier in Lancashire. Already renowned for his Tamburlaine, he would be rivalled only by Richard Burbage as the leading tragedian on the Elizabethan stage; in partnership with Henslowe, whose stepdaughter he married in 1592, Alleyn grew rich enough to found Dulwich College, where his letters and Henslowe's account-books were unearthed in 1790.

But Shakespeare's first London patron was James Burbage, who had been

(OPPOSITE)
OPHELIA AND LAERTES
FROM 'HAMLET'.
PAINTING BY
WILLIAM GORDON WILLS
1828–91.

leading theatrical troupes to Stratford since as long ago as 1573, when his new recruit was just nine years old. The father of Richard, the actor who would create most of the great Shakespearean roles, this genial impresario was the kind of man to have befriended the stagestruck son of the former mayor, inviting him to look him up if ever he fetched up in London in need of work. It was at Burbage's Shoreditch Theatre, we know, that Shakespeare the actor would eventually play the Ghost in a production of his own *Hamlet*. But how did he make his start in the theatre?

Since 1583 Burbage's Theatre had been the London base of the Queen's Men, with whom we have seen Shakespeare arrive in London. Next door was a slaughter-house, where there would be work for a butcher's apprentice. All the traditions stress that the newlywed father was 'poor', 'without money and friends', at the 'extreme end of ruin', forced to endure a 'very low degree of drudgery'. According to an early eighteenth-century biographer, he was 'received into the company then in being, at first in a very mean rank; but his admirable wit, and the natural turn of it to the stage, soon distinguished him, if not as an extraordinary actor, yet as an excellent writer.'

Ten years earlier, at the end of the century in which Shakespeare died, another memoirist recorded that he was 'first received into the playhouse as a serviture'. But in what role, exactly? Later references to the playwright as a 'rude groom' appear to confirm the intriguing tradition that Shakespeare first found employment by combining the role of ostler (or stableman), looking after the 'better sort of' theatregoers' horses, with part-time actor and backstage factotum. So says, for instance, no less an authority than Samuel Johnson. But if Shakespeare invented a lucrative sixteenth-century version of valet parking, he seems also to have moonlighted backstage during performances, while his 'boys' tended the horses, as an apprentice prompter. According to his first biographer, Rowe, Shakespeare's 'first office in the theatre was that of prompter's attendant, whose employment it is to give the performers notice to be ready to enter, as often as the business of the play requires their appearance on the stage.' More likely, this was promotion for the ostler – bringing him inside the theatre, where he really wanted to be, if as yet backstage.

A SKETCH OF THE SWAN THEATRE
IN LONDON.
DRAWING BY JOHANN DE WITT.

The role of prompter would have been a handy start, not least at rehearsals, when Shakespeare would have been required to 'stand in' from time to time, and given a chance to show off what talents he had as an actor. From there, it was but a short step to minor roles, even understudying bigger ones. Given his apparent limitations as a performer, it was only natural that the rural poet, the Plautus of his schooldays still fresh in his mind, would also turn his hand to writing. A jobbing playwright who could fill in onstage, taking on the occasional minor role, would seem a very useful acquisition to any troupe. To Shakespeare, for his part, membership of the Queen's Players was the perfect start to his career – with the leading company of the moment, regularly commanded to perform at court.

The Queen's troupe, recruited at Elizabeth's personal command, appeared frequently at court during the first season of its existence, 1583–84, while earning its keep before paying audiences at Burbage's Theatre. Precisely when Shakespeare signed on is unknown; his name is not among the dozen licensed by the City Corporation in November 1583 to play 'at the sign of the Bull in Bishopsgate Street and the sign of the Bull in Gracechurch Street and nowhere else within this city.' Among those who were was the star comedian of the moment, Richard Tarleton, whose memory lingered fondly with Shakespeare when he conjured Hamlet's touching memories of Yorick. So Tarleton's death in 1588 suggests that the poet had joined the Queen's Men by

that date; the mention of his name in an early eighteenth-century woodcut as 'one of the first actors in Shakespeare's plays' further suggests that the new recruit was already contributing new or revised dramas to the company's repertoire.

Shakespeare's first known London address was in Westminster, nearer the court than the playhouses. The Folger Library in Washington DC possesses a copy of a legal textbook entitled *Archaionomia*, edited by William Lambarde and published in 1568, on which is inscribed the name 'Wm Shakespeare'. In the same volume appears a note, presumably added by a later owner: 'Mr. Wm Shakespeare lived at No. 1 Little Crown St. Westminster NB near Dorset Steps, St James's Park'.

Why was Shakespeare living so far from the theatrical action? The rent may, perhaps, have been cheaper; but legal records show that in early 1589 he and his parents were pursuing through a Westminster law-court their continuing claim against his cousin John Lambert for restoration of their rights in the

A VIEW OF WESTMINSTER
FROM THE RIVER THAMES.
UNATTRIBUTED
ENGRAVING, 1647.

(PAGES 104–105)
THE ACTORS BEFORE
HAMLET, 1875.
PAINTING BY
LADISLAS VON
CZACHORSKI
1850–1911.

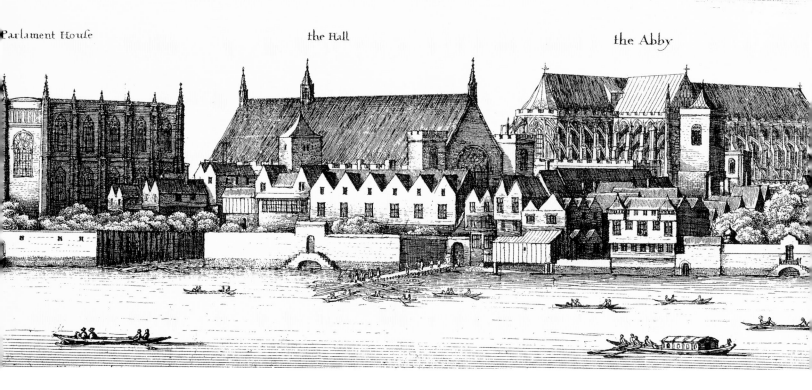

Parlament House   the Hall   the Abby

Asbies estate. They would eventually lose their suit, and thus his patrimony; but in the process he appears to have mastered the art of the scrivener, or lawyer's copy-clerk. The handwriting of Shakespeare's signature on the book suggests as much; and we have the word of a contemporary, Nashe, that some playwrights of the day lived some distance from the literary heart of London, making a 'peripatetical' path to the playhouses and booksellers in the 'inner parts of the city'.

Was Shakespeare sharing digs with his fellow grammar-school boy, Thomas Kyd, chuckling defiantly over the envious attacks of the university-educated Nashe? Were the two country hicks stitching together a crude revenge tragedy about a Danish prince called Hamlet – now lost, but known to have enjoyed a certain success in the late 1580s? Both would have admired (and learnt, if not indeed stolen, from) Marlowe's *Tamburlaine*. As for the rest of the 'University Wits', it would seem in character for Shakespeare to come home from the Theatre, well-lubricated with ale, and mock the clunking lines declaimed around him that afternoon, vowing to improve on them in his own work-in-progress.

As a member of the Queen's Company, both on the road and in town, he would have become familiar with several anonymous plays then in their repertoire which would later echo, in revised and vastly refined form, through his own. Apart from *The Troublesome Reign of King John*, *The Famous Victories of Henry the Fifth*, and *The True Chronicle of King Leir, and his three daughters* – three works of unknown authorship in which Shakespeare may well have had a hand – the Queen's Men did good business with a play called *Felix and Philomena*, first performed before their patron, the Queen herself, at Greenwich in January 1585. The text they played – no doubt cobbled together by the cast themselves, as was often the case before they acquired their own in-house playwright – was based on a work of Montemayor written in Spanish in 1542, translated into French in 1578, entitled *Felix and Felismena*. This was clearly one of Shakespeare's prime sources for his own early comedy, *The Two Gentlemen of Verona*.

But comedy could wait, as indeed could tragedy. *Titus Andronicus* is undoubtedly an early work, placed by some scholars at the very start of his playwriting career, but now broadly accepted as later than the ostler's first, at times primitive forays into stagecraft. History plays were the box-office phenomenon of the moment; and it was with a history cycle quite without precedent that Shakespeare appears first to have proposed himself to his fellows as a better writer than actor. The Queen's Men, it seems, had yet to be convinced, moving Shakespeare the writer — if not the actor — to turn free-lance. They would later, of course, perform his plays regularly, as would all the troupes who could lay their hands on them; but his first efforts found their real success in the version staged by the players employed by the Derby family, with whom he had first made that early connection in Lancashire — and whose recent ancestors, craftily enough, it glorified.

'How it would have joyed brave Talbot (the terror of the French)', wrote Nashe in 1592, 'to think that after he had lain two hundred years in the tomb, he should triumph again on the stage, and have his bones embalmed with the tears of ten thousand spectators at least (at several times), who, in the trage-dian who represents his person, behold him fresh bleeding.' Unless he is to be taken at face value, the envious Nashe may have been drawing ironic attention to Shakespeare's rewriting of history in the aggrandisement of the role of the House of Derby in the Wars of the Roses. And it was Strange's players who brought the *Henry VI* cycle its biggest triumph, establishing the actor-turned-playwright as a force on the London stage.

On Saturday 19 February the 1592 Rose season of Lord Strange's Men, led by Alleyn, got off to a mediocre start. Robert Greene's comedy, *Friar Bacon and Friar Bungay*, only half-filled the theatre, as did that week's cycle of anonymous plays: *Muly Mulocco*, *The Spanish Comedy of Don Horatio*, *Sir John Mandeville* and *Harry of Cornwall*. The following Saturday, 26 February, business picked up with a packed house for Marlowe's *The Jew of Malta*. But even that was surpassed by a history play first performed the following Friday, 3 March, which proved the best box-office draw of the season. 'Harey the vj £3.16.8.' recorded Henslowe in his account-book.

According to Nashe, more than ten thousand people saw Shakespeare's first full history cycle at the Rose that summer. 'The takings continue high,' purrs Henslowe's diary for 5 April, after further performances on the 7, 11, 16 and 28 March; so he scheduled fourteen more during April, May and June. The various rival theatrical troupes had been living through turbulent times, making it hard for posterity to track the stage provenance of Shakespeare's early works. From the title-page of a published version *of 3 Henry VI*, we know that it had been 'oft enacted' by the Earl of Pembroke's Men, who also had *Titus Andronicus* in their repertoire. But this does not tell us much. Copyright in plays rested not with the playwright but the company who commissioned them; pirate versions abounded, even in print; actors who defected to other companies were bribed to come up with 'memorial reconstructions', or inevitably defective versions put together from their memory of other parts as well as their own — thus combining with the mistakes and improvisations of compositors to bequeath the Shakespeare industry a bottomless pit of textual problems to argue over till doomsday.

In 1590, we do know, Strange's servants and the Admiral's Men merged under the leadership of Alleyn, using the two Shoreditch playhouses, Burbage's Theatre and its annexe, the Curtain. In May 1591 Alleyn fell out with Burbage, boldly leading his troupe across the river to Henslowe's Rose, where they found a new lease of life as Lord Strange's Men. But not all of Alleyn's colleagues followed him; seeing himself as a rival to Alleyn's thespian laurels, Burbage's son Richard persuaded some players to stay behind with him in Shoreditch, where they formed a new company under the patronage of the Earl of Pembroke. Then

SERENADE IN FRONT OF JULIA'S WINDOW, FROM 'THE TWO GENTLEMEN OF VERONA'. COLOUR LITHOGRAPH BY JOHN GILBERT C.1860.

aged twenty-three, four years younger than Shakespeare, Richard Burbage would in time create the roles of Richard III, Hamlet, Othello and Lear; he it was, more than Shakespeare, who would maintain a lifelong association with Pembroke, ended only by the actor's death in 1619, after which the theatre-loving earl could no longer bring himself to visit the playhouse where his 'old acquaintance' had trod the boards.

Shakespeare's own connections with Pembroke — believed by some to be the 'fair youth' of the cycle of sonnets on which he would soon embark — may be surmised from the fact that the fellow-actors who collected his plays after his death, and published the First Folio in 1623, chose to dedicate the volume to him. It is possible that Pembroke's Men began life as an offshoot of the Queen's Men, given their irregular employment and the frequent dispersals caused by outbreaks of the plague. There was, for sure, a special bond between the freelance dramatist, also an actor in Burbage's company, and the young nobleman who now paid their wages; such records as we have suggest that his plays were performed more often by Pembroke's Men than by any other company. But the Master of the Revels was more concerned with maintaining public decency than enforcing the rudimentary laws of copyright. Shakespeare's plays, like all plays, did the rounds.

Given the scale and range of his eventual output, it seems wholly in character that Shakespeare chose to begin his work as a playwright with an ambitious tetralogy covering fifty years of comparatively recent British history — a theatrical feat never previously attempted, in a style which, while still rudimentary, was quite unlike anything that had gone before. By assigning character and motives, thoughts and feelings to historical figures still fresh in the national mind, and by holding them (rather than divine will) responsible for the consequences of their own actions, Shakespeare joined Marlowe in breaking free of the plodding, one-dimensional archetypes of the morality and mystery plays of the mediaeval tradition.

The historical King Henry VI (1421–71) was a pale shadow of his heroic, belligerent father, Henry V, to whom Shakespeare would return in due course. A child when he succeeded to the throne, Henry remained as impotent in adulthood in the face of the disputes among the rival noblemen jockeying for position in the absence of his supreme authority. In Shakespeare's scheme of things, reworking the 1587 edition of Holinshed's *Chronicles* and numerous lesser sources, the King remains a mere spectator in his own sad history, powerless to prevent the loss of France, the fall of Gloucester, the rise of York, the disintegration of his kingdom into virtual anarchy — even, eventually, his own death. In Part 3, symbolically, he is even powerless to speak, twice demanding his say and twice being denied it. This, to an Elizabethan audience, was the ultimate heresy against the divinity that still did hedge a king.

(OPPOSITE)
HAMLET AND HORATIO
IN THE GRAVEYARD.
PAINTING BY EUGENE
DELACROIX, 1799–1863.

The cycle traces the long, slow decline of England after the death of its warrior-king, Henry V, as the collapse of his French conquests and the erosion of royal power leads inexorably to the dynastic squabbles that result in civil war. From the outset, with Henry's noblemen already arguing about the succession, Shakespeare has in mind an exploration of cause and effect on a vast, panoramic scale. To Shakespeare, Henry VI's reign was a vacuum in which to explore the onset of chaos and disorder. These would remain abiding themes, still to the fore in his most mature tragedies, as would the humanity with which he endowed the unfortunate monarch, who grows gradually more eloquent as his fortunes decline.

The brash self-confidence of youth is apparent throughout the cycle, with its vast epic sweep, its huge cast of characters, its preference for pageantry and action over agonised introspection, and above all its high, sententious style, in which the many and various voices are barely differentiated. There are honourable exceptions, such as the idiomatic prose of the Jack Cade sequence, and the emotional power of Young Clifford's verse on discovering the corpse of his father, both in Part 2. And there are thematic portents of the greater Shakespeare to come: the collapse of civic order, for instance, mirrored in that of families at war with themselves, brother plotting to kill brother, humanity reduced to the amoral anarchy of animals and the elements.

Part 3 also sees the emergence of a character quite distinct from the rest, a 'heap of wrath, a foul indigested lump' for whom Shakespeare clearly had further plans. 'Why,' he grins, 'I can smile, and murther whiles I smile.' Our first sight of Richard, Duke of Gloucester seems to transport the poet into a new dimension, as if he were already writing his next play, the logical conclusion of the tetralogy. *Richard III* picks up where *3 Henry VI* left off, with Gloucester plotting at the dead king's funeral. In his celebrated opening speech – 'Now is the winter of our discontent / Made glorious summer by this son of York' – lie the seeds of the great soliloquies to come. Richard's wry explanation of his decision to play the villain is more of an extended aside than a soliloquy; but it carries the early hallmarks of the self-knowledge (or lack of it, leading to self-questioning) which would wring from Shakespeare some of his supreme moments. Richard's bitter eloquence in analysing his own villainy anticipates

(OPPOSITE)
PORTRAIT OF THE ACTOR
WILLIAM POWELL,
1735–69, AS POSTHUMOUS
IN 'CYMBELINE', C.1765.
PAINTING BY
FRANCIS WHEATLEY,
1747–1801.

Iago's much more interesting failure to do so, and Macbeth's paranoid ambivalence.

If Ned Alleyn had made Shakespeare's first big part his own, coining it for himself and Henslowe as Henry VI, it was Richard Burbage (and thus Pembroke's Men) who cornered the sequel, as we know from a rare, if uncorroborated Shakespeare anecdote. On 13 March 1601 a barrister of the Middle Temple named John Manningham entered the following note in his diary:

> *Upon a time when Burbage played Richard III, there was a citizen grew so far in liking with him, that before she went from the play she appointed him to come that night unto her by the name of Richard the Third. Shakespeare, overhearing their conversation, went before, was entertained and at his game ere Burbage came.*
>
> *Then, message being brought that Richard III was at the door, Shakespeare caused return to be made that William the Conqueror was before Richard the Third.*

This, for Shakespeare biographers, is one of those unverifiable vignettes too good to discard on the grounds of merely dubious provenance. It conjures up the roistering Bard of the popular, wishful-thinking imagination, the Bard who would later suffer at least one dose of the clap, living the hell-raising London life of his most earthy, engaging characters, with his wife and children at a safe distance in Stratford — the irrepressible, fun-loving Bard who, sooner or later, had to turn his hand to comedy.

At the end of 1589 the poet Edmund Spenser, who spent most of his life in Ireland, returned to his native London for an audience with the Queen. He also took the chance to entrust to the printer the first three books of his majestic epic *The Faerie Queene*, evidently admired by Shakespeare, who pays it due tribute in *Love's Labour's Lost*. Now, within a year of his visit, the other great poet of the age appears to have repaid the compliment. In *The Teares of the Muses*, registered in December 1590, Spenser bemoaned the current neglect of comedy on the London stage — with two honourable exceptions. One was a player who had recently

TITLE PAGE OF SPENSER'S
'THE FAERIE QUEENE', 1590.

THE FAERIE
QVEENE.

Difposed into twelue books,
Fashioning
XII. Morall vertues.

LONDON
Printed for William Ponfonbie.
1590.

died – clearly a reference to Dick Tarleton – while the other was a writer, a 'gentle Spirit',

> *from whose pen*
> *Large streams of honey and sweet nectar flow,*
> *Scorning the boldness of such base-born men,*
> *Which dare their follies forth so rashly throw…*

If Spenser had seen a Shakespeare comedy before 1590, which one? On purely stylistic grounds the prime suspect would be *The Two Gentlemen of Verona*, the least sophisticated of all Shakespeare's comedies, believed to have been performed by the early 1590s. Its stagecraft is uniquely primitive, with few scenes accommodating more than two or three speaking roles, while its dénouement is notoriously inept. Few audiences of any age have been able to stomach the abrupt generosity of one Gentleman, Valentine, in forgiving the amorous treachery of the other, Proteus, by relinquishing his own true love as a supreme gesture of friendship. Again, a woman is being treated as a mere chattel, with no say in her own destiny. And there is no sense at all of place; we might as well be in Bankside as Verona, for all the topographical colours this eventual master of the Italian palette brings to his canvas. He would soon make amends in *Romeo and Juliet*, where the swords of young aristocrats flash in the sun with rather more localised resonance.

In a play about the respective claims of love and friendship, moreover, the most steadfast (and touching) relationship in the entire piece is that between Launce, the rough-hewn prototype of all Shakespearean clowns, and his mangy dog Crab – who all too often, all too easily, steals the show. As recently as 1986 the Oxford editors boldly adjudged *The Two Gentlemen of Verona* to be Shakespeare's first play, placing it even before the *Henry VI* cycle, again on stylistic grounds; its dramatic structure being 'comparatively unambitious', and its construction betraying 'an uncertainty of technique suggestive of inexperience', the play could be seen as 'a dramatic laboratory in which Shakespeare first experimented with conventions of romantic comedy which he would later treat with a more subtle complexity'.

The Arden editor claims the same privilege for *The Taming of the Shrew*, while others make a case for *The Comedy of Errors* as Shakespeare's first play. But

both show signs of much more experienced stagecraft, and lie naturally with *Love's Labour's Lost* in the great comic burst ahead, after a poetic interlude, in 1593–94. First, he had to produce his own version of the Senecan revenge tragedy so much in vogue at the time – to fulfil his experimentation, in this first full flowering of his youthful talent, with all three of the genres – history, comedy, tragedy – that would shape his entire career and constitute the formal sub-divisions of his posthumously collected works.

Towards the end of his *Henry VI* trilogy, Shakespeare stages the murder of York standing on a molehill with a crown of paper on his head. The famous scene builds to a crescendo of violence so intense that 'horror turns to pity'. The same might be said of *Titus Andronicus*, recorded as 'new' in Henslowe's log when staged at the Rose by Sussex's Men on 20 January 1594. But 'new' need not be taken to mean newly written; if not merely an abbreviation for 'Newington Butts', the south London site of one of his theatres, it could signify newly licensed, or else a revision by the author or simply a new production. When *Titus* was published later that year, the title-page asserts that this 'Most Lamentable Roman Tragedy' had been performed by 'the Right Honourable the Earl of Derby, Earl of Pembroke, and Earl of Sussex their Servants'. This latest performance by Sussex's Men at the Rose, therefore, was but the latest in a long line of a popular play dating back several years.

Did Shakespeare intend his own Grand Guignol version of the revenge tradition as a homage to Kyd and Marlowe, or a grotesque parody? Amid other horrors, two brothers rape Titus's daughter Lavinia on the corpse of her husband, whom they have murdered, then cut out her tongue and sever her hands to prevent her revealing their names. When she traces them in the earth, with a stick clasped between her stumps, Titus kills the brothers, grinds their bones to flour, and cooks them in a pie which he serves to their mother. Only two of the play's central characters survive its dénouement, after which one sentences the other to be buried waist-deep and starved to death.

Titus has always been notoriously hard going for both cast and audiences; if not laughed off the stage, it requires extra paramedics to cope with the number of fainting spectators. *Titus Andronicus* was surely written with the box-

(OPPOSITE)
RICHARD III.
UNKNOWN ARTIST.

office in mind, and it proved a huge success; the play was very popular in Shakespeare's lifetime, appearing in three editions between 1594 and 1611. Its verse is often lumpen, the structure episodic and the action surreal; but *Titus Andronicus* remains, at worst, the least of Shakespeare's achievements in a new genre he was to make his own, of lasting value as an interim milestone between the revenge tradition and *Hamlet*.

So by 1592 Shakespeare had written at least five, perhaps seven plays — more, if you accept the passionate arguments for the admission to the canon of a play called *Edmund Ironside*. The Stratford man seems more likely to have had a collaborative hand in *Edward III*, at least some of which is now accepted by the editors of several of the standard editions of the *Collected Works*. But the summer of 1592 brought an outbreak of the plague so severe that London's theatres were summarily closed. To the Church, the theatres themselves were nothing less than the cause of the plague. In the brutal logic of one Puritan preacher at Paul's Cross: 'The cause of plague is sin, if you look to it well; and the cause of sin are plays: therefore the cause of plague are plays.' To the authorities, not unreasonably, any kind of public congregation, such as that attracted by the theatres, was undesirable; given the unsavoury lifestyle of many groundlings, 'infected with sores running on them', theatres were 'perilous for contagion'. As the death-toll grew alarmingly towards the end of 1592, the Privy Council stepped in to suspend 'all manner of concourse and public meetings of the people at plays, bear-baitings, bowlings and other like assemblies' within a seven-mile radius of London — apart, of course, from church services.

For the various troupes of players, deprived of their livelihood, the indefinite closure of London's theatres was disastrous. As most left the capital, forced to tour in *ad hoc* groups, Shakespeare decided he had better things to do. Plays, after all, were ephemeral effusions, rarely revived once the box-office failed, printed only by pirates exploiting the law's failure to protect what was laughably called copyright. Poetry was the vocation of the true writer, and his best hope of immortality. So it was to poetry that he turned his hand during this theatrical interregnum, while his fellows ground their weary, unhappy way around the provincial inn-yard circuit.

(OPPOSITE)
HENRY VI.
UNKNOWN ARTIST.

HENRY THE SIXTH

V

THE 'UPSTART CROW'

1592–1594

Of all young Shakespeare's contemporaries
in literary London, none was more jealous
of his early precocity than Robert Greene,
the most bohemian of the university-
educated writers. The author of five plays,
as well as numerous poems and pamphlets,
he was only some four years older
than the new, 'unschooled' arrival on the
theatrical scene.

By the time the theatres reopened, just as he was enjoying the success of his first major narrative poem, Shakespeare found his name also made as a playwright by the deathbed insult of a tired, jealous rival, a worn-out, drunken wreck of a writer reaching the end of both his tether and his mortal span. In *A Groatsworth of Witte, boughte with a million of Repentance*, an actor at work in the London theatre 'for seven years space' came in for thunderous abuse from the satirist Robert Greene, who accused him *inter alia* of being in love with the sound of his own voice, which had 'terribly thundered' from the stage. The object of Greene's wrath remains unidentified. But it was clearly the same actor-turned-writer whom he nicknames 'Shake-scene' earlier in the same document, thus bequeathing posterity its first surviving mention of Shakespeare's presence in London as a playwright.

Of all young Shakespeare's contemporaries in literary London, none was more jealous of his early precocity than Greene, the most bohemian of the university-educated writers. The author of five plays, as well as numerous poems and pamphlets, he was only some four years older than the new, 'unschooled' arrival on the theatrical scene. In September 1592, left behind by his actor-friends when the plague again drove them out of town, Greene lay dying of the pox (i.e. syphilis) in squalid poverty. In his early thirties, separated from his long-suffering wife Dorothea, he shared his filthy, rat-ridden London hovel with a distraught, nagging mistress, the sister of a disreputable acolyte 'Cutting' Ball. Greene's last days saw him obsessed with the absent players – those greedy, script-hungry parasites who fastened on his fellow playwrights, gullible scholars all, and bled them dry for paltry rewards. There they were now, far from the horrors of plague-ridden London, growing fat on provincial profits due to the literary hands that fed them. 'Trust them not,' Greene warned his fellow playwrights – primarily Nashe, Peele and Marlowe. One in particular, who had the nerve to show pretensions as a writer, he singled out for sarcastic denunciation:

> *There is an upstart crow, beautified with our feathers, that with his*
> *'Tiger's heart wrapt in a player's hide' supposes he is well able to*
> *bombast out a blank verse as the best of you; and being an absolute*
> *Johannes factotum, is in his own conceit the only Shake-scene in a country.*

'Oh that I might entreat your rare wits to be employed in more profitable courses,' the dying writer begged his friends, 'and let those apes imitate your past excellence, and never more acquaint them with your admired inventions.'

The 'upstart crow' was, of course, Shakespeare. His 'tiger's heart wrapt in a player's hide' was a sneering echo of a celebrated line in *The True Tragedy*, alias *3 Henry VI*. The young arriviste appears to have contented himself with a complaint to the deceased's printer, Henry Chettle, provoking a prompt and fawning apology that December. Clearly rattled by the offence he had caused Shakespeare, on whose behalf people in high places had interceded to powerful effect, Chettle now found him as 'upright' and 'honest' a man as he was 'excellent' and 'graceful' a writer.

It may safely be assumed that the 'divers of worship' who had so put the wind up the reckless publisher included Henry Wriothesley, 3rd Earl of Southampton, who had decided to become Shakespeare's patron. No wonder Greene, Nashe and the rest were quite so exercised about the 'upstart crow'. Just when they were all in need of money, he had wormed his way into the lucrative affections of the man best placed to offer it – the man whose patronage they had all been seeking. Greene and Nashe would both offer dedications to Southampton, but it was Shakespeare with whom the young earl had begun to develop a relationship, both professional and personal, of striking intensity.

At the age of twenty-eight, after at least five years in London, Shakespeare was well-established as an actor and playwright. In the autumn of 1592, as the plague appeared to ebb, his fellow-players returned to the capital; but the cold winter had bought merely a temporary reprieve, and the theatres closed down again on 2 February. They were to remain closed throughout most of 1593, as the disease claimed more than 11,000 lives – at its height, a thousand a week. After a brief winter reopening, they were closed again in February 1594, reopened in April, then again shut down that summer. This proved the longest closure yet, threatening the fragile stability of most troupes, which disintegrated under the pressures of provincial touring. When the plague finally abated, most had to start again from scratch.

Shakespeare chose to stay behind in London. With the theatres indefi-

(OPPOSITE)
DESDEMONA AND EMILIA
FROM 'OTHELLO' 1867.
PAINTING BY
DANIEL MACLISE,
1806–70.

nitely closed, he bade his thespian colleagues an open-ended farewell as they headed off to the provinces, while he remained behind with the express intention of making his name as a poet. By doing so, of course, he ran the considerable risk that the plague might cut short a distinctly promising career; having survived it in infancy, however, he was still young enough to be capable of believing that he led a charmed life. Besides, returning to Stratford, to ride out the crisis and write poems amid the distractions of a noisy, hard-pressed household, was not an attractive option. With no theatrical income, he had to cast around for a patron. And now, to the malicious envy of Greene and Nashe, the country boy seemed to have found one.

JOHN FLORIO.
ENGRAVING BY W. HOLE.

Did it help, perhaps, that the handsome young Earl of Southampton – still only nineteen, nine years younger than Shakespeare – also came from a staunchly Catholic family, distantly related to that of the poet's mother? If the family connection were not reason enough for nobleman and poet to meet, they might well have known each other from one of the playhouses, a regular haunt of members of the Inns of Court, where Southampton had been sent after graduating from Cambridge at the age of sixteen. Or they may have been introduced by John Florio, the immigrant Italian scholar who also frequented the theatres while compiling his Anglo-Italian dictionary, *A World of Words* (1598). Florio was Southampton's secretary, giving the lie to frequent suggestions that Shakespeare himself held this post. But the Italian word-lover and the Warwickshire word-spinner were undoubtedly acquainted; the Italian proverb quoted by Holofernes in *Love's Labour's Lost* suggests that the character is in part an affectionate caricature of the Italian scholar who introduced Shakespeare, with such spectacular effect, to the works of Montaigne.

Southampton and Shakespeare would swiftly have discovered dangerous matters of mutual concern to discuss in discreet corners. Back in Stratford, William's father was still flouting the religious laws; twice that year, in March

(OPPOSITE)
FALSTAFF ENACTING
'HENRY IV', C.1834.
PAINTING BY
GEORGE WHITING FLAGG,
1816–97.

PHILIPVS SYDNEYVS
AN ÆTATIS 23.

CÆTERA FAMA~
E D

and September, John Shakespeare's name appeared among lists of recusants who 'refused obstinately' to attend church 'for fear of process from debt'. At court, meanwhile, the elegant and erudite Southampton may have been a favourite of the Queen, but he was forging political and religious alliances which would eventually land him in trouble.

The earl's father, a Catholic zealot whose own beliefs had seen him sent to the Tower, had died in 1581, leaving his eight-year-old son and heir a royal ward, entrusted to the guardianship of William Cecil, Lord Burghley, Lord High Treasurer of England. Over the past two years, since coming to London from Cambridge, Southampton had come under pressure from both Burghley and his mother to marry, with a view to ensuring the succession to his title. Now his grandfather, too, weighed in — another peer of the realm, Lord Montacute (these days spelt Montague) of Beaulieu. As he entered Southampton's circle, Shakespeare composed a cycle of seventeen sonnets urging a handsome young man to marry, primarily for the sake of reproducing his own physical charms. Although they brought a bold new dimension to the current vogue for love-sonnets, most recently exemplified by Sir Philip Sidney's much tamer cycle, *Astrophel and Stella* (which appeared posthumously in 1591), Shakespeare's sonnets were never intended for publication.

But his next poem, about a beautiful young man resisting the advances of an importunate woman, certainly was. He returned to the *Metamorphoses* of his beloved Ovid for the subject-matter of his first long venture into narrative poetry, prefacing it with an extravagant dedication to Southampton. The volume was printed by Richard Field, Shakespeare's friend and contemporary from Stratford, who had had the good sense to marry the widow of his French Master, Thomas Vautrollier, thus inheriting the business. As their professional partnership developed, rumour would have it that Shakespeare himself performed Field's 'office 'twixt his sheets' — no doubt while his old friend was on a trip home to Stratford, cheerfully bearing Shakespeare's greetings to his own family. As yet, however, it seems to have been purely a professional relationship — and a very successful one: *Venus and Adonis* was to enjoy nine reprints in his lifetime — the Elizabethan equivalent of a bestseller — and six more within twenty years of his death.

The poem's covert references to Roman Catholicism would have pleased Southampton as much as Adonis' indifference to Venus' advances. The next batch of sonnets, 18–39, probably written at much the same time, reverse the young earl's dilemma with even more eloquent expressions of unrequited love, presumably on behalf of an actual or imaginary suitor. The first, 'Shall I compare thee to a summer's day?' is but the best-known of a transcendent sequence moving on from the 'need-to-breed' theme to some of the most exquisite love lyrics ever written, often introspective about the power of love to inspire verse.

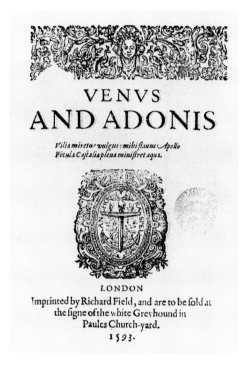

TITLE PAGE OF SHAKESPEARE'S FIRST PUBLISHED WORK, THE NARRATIVE POEM 'VENUS AND ADONIS', 1593.

Although still addressed to the 'fair youth', presumably Southampton, these sonnets should not be taken – as they so often are – to suggest that Shakespeare himself was homosexual. If these private poems are, to some extent, unavoidably about himself – 'with this key,' wrote Wordsworth, 'Shakespeare unlocked his heart' – Sonnet 20 makes the poet's heterosexuality brutally, if reluctantly, clear. With a pun on 'prick' – one of many such references to male and female genitalia throughout the cycle, nothing untoward for an Elizabethan sonneteer – the poet specifically laments the fact that the penis of his effeminate young 'master-mistress' is of no physical use to him.

Shakespeare would explore homosexuality elsewhere, as in *The Merchant of Venice*, where the love of the merchant Antonio for his friend Bassanio is threatened by the wealthy Portia's quest for a husband. Elizabethan 'love' between men anyway functioned at several removes from Plato; figures as lusty as Falstaff or as macho as Coriolanus use the word 'lover' to denote a male friend. But any such ambiguity soon disappears from the Sonnets, where by 40–42 the poet appears to fear that the male object of his admiration has stolen his own female lover. In 78–86 he suspects that his place in the young man's affections has been usurped by another, superior poet – the so-called 'rival poet' of interminable scholarly speculation, perhaps Marlowe, more likely Chapman.

(PAGES 130–131)
OTHELLO RELATING HIS ADVENTURES.
PAINTING BY ROBERT ALEXANDER HILLINGFORD, 1825–1904.
(OPPOSITE)
KATHERINA, FROM 'TAMING OF THE SHREW', 1896.
PAINTING BY EDWARD ROBERT HUGHES, 1851–1914.

Did Shakespeare fear the loss of Southampton's patronage to his university-educated rival, the only contemporary for whose work he had much respect? If so, the problem appears to have been solved within the year, on the publication of his second long narrative poem. Entered in the Stationers Register on 9 May 1594, thirteen months after *Venus and Adonis*, *The 'Ravyshment' of Lucrece* amounts to the 'graver labour' Shakespeare had promised Southampton. Again printed by Richard Field – but this time for a different publisher, John Harrison, to whom he now also consigned the earlier poem – the quarto bears only the word Lucrece on its title-page, while the running-heads have changed 'Ravyshment' to Rape. As with *Venus and Adonis*, Shakespeare himself seems to have corrected the proofs and taken an interest in every stage of production – a care, it is worth remembering, which he never lavished upon any of his plays.

While he was writing *The Rape of Lucrece*, as the plague raged through the streets of London, Shakespeare was probably living in the comfortable *cordon sanitaire* of Southampton House in Holborn, the earl's London home (or perhaps at his country seat at Titchfield, Hampshire). Over these two plague-ridden years he was at work on two, perhaps three more comedies for the stage as well as continuing to pour out sonnets for himself, his patron and their intimate circle.

The last twenty-eight, 127–154, are addressed to a woman, a dark-skinned woman, whose identity has tantalised four centuries of scholars. 'Whoever she was, she enchanted the poet with her beauty and fiery passion, then tormented him with her infidelity,' as one scholar has racily put it. 'But great passion makes for great poetry. He wouldn't have been Shakespeare if he'd stayed quietly at home with Anne Hathaway. In the bed department, she was second best.'

Shakespeare would surely have been amused by the passion aroused among habitually passionless scholars by the identity of his 'Dark Lady'. This same current authority, Jonathan Bate, has recently argued the claims of John Florio's wife, forename unknown, sister of the poet Samuel Daniel. 'You *must* believe in Mrs Florio,' he pleads (paraphrasing Oscar Wilde). 'I almost do myself ... ' To be 'accounted most fair', according to Florio himself, a woman must have 'black eyes, black brows, black hairs'. But we have no idea what Mrs

(OPPOSITE)
FERDINAND DISARMED
BY THE MAGIC OF
PROSPERO, FROM
'THE TEMPEST'.
PAINTING BY WILLIAM
HAMILTON, 1750–1801.

Florio looked like, any more than we do Emilia Lanier, the 'definitive … unanswerable' solution of the late A. L. Rowse, self-styled 'leading authority on the age in which Shakespeare lived and wrote', who swatted dissent aside as 'complete rubbish' from 'inferior minds'.

There may seem more than a hint of racism in the assumption that a 'dark lady' must be of continental origin or connections; yet, as Bate himself observes, in Elizabethan love literature 'fairness and darkness have a great deal more to do with social status than with actual hair and eye colour.' So should we be looking further down the social scale? Other suspects have included Lucy Negro, notorious, dark-skinned Clerkenwell prostitute – not to be confused with Lucy Morgan, once one of the Queen's ladies-in-waiting, later a brothel-keeper.

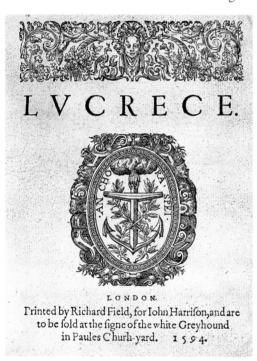

But textual hints appear to support Rowse's insistence that the Dark Lady was 'a well known person … of superior social standing to Shakespeare'. This would enhance the claims of Penelope Rich, born Lady Penelope Devereux, sister of the Earl of Essex, and the original 'Stella' of Sidney's own sonnet cycle, *Astrophel and Stella*. Or Mary ('Mall') Fitton, maid of honour to the Queen, impregnated by the Earl of Pembroke, and lusted after by her father's lecherous friend Sir William Knollys, Controller of the Queen's Household, whom the poet supposedly caricatured as Malvolio (as in 'I want Mall').

In the end, as so often, posterity is left groping around in the shadows of Shakespeare, who has left us another enigma as elusive as allusive, to the point where all attempts to solve it can only wind up demeaning the rare poetry from which it springs. Perhaps it is best, with Anthony Burgess, to leave the Dark Lady 'anonymous, even composite', an immortal icon of 'some of the commonest experiences known to men – obsession with a woman's body, revulsion, pain in desertion, resignation at another's treachery' not to mention 'the irresistible lure of the primal darkness that resides in all women, whether white or black'.

(OPPOSITE)
LADY PENELOPE RICH,
LATER LADY DEVONSHIRE,
C.1562–1607.
UNKNOWN ARTIST.

Better, even, to think of the Dark Lady in Shakespeare's own fictional terms — as that prototype of Shakespeare's many assertive women, Rosaline in *Love's Labour's Lost*, the 'whitely wanton with a velvet brow', with dark 'pitchballs' for eyes, who has much the same plans for Berowne as had the Dark Lady for the poet of the Sonnets. In which case we must also cast Southampton as the King of Navarre, affecting to elevate scholarship over sex, and Shakespeare himself as the eloquent, skirt-chasing Berowne. For the French court setting read Southampton's equally cultured, if playful household, where the study (and production) of literature was constantly interrupted by amorous intrigues.

If it was originally written at the same time as the Sonnets, and equally full of in-jokes and double entendres about the goings-on in Southampton's circle, can it be any coincidence that *Love's Labour's Lost* is the first of only three plays for which Shakespeare plucked the plot, if not from thin air, from no other primary source? The refined literary style and elaborate wordplay of his most heavily-rhymed play amount almost to a homage to Sidney, with distant echoes of Lyly; and its 'open' ending (the longest scene in all Shakespeare) recalls Chaucer's *The Parliament of Fowles*. But the setting and framework sprang — as with his last solo work, *The Tempest* — from a contemporary event, in this case a diplomatic mission to Aquitaine during the recent French civil war, which ended in 1593 with the King of Navarre becoming King Henri IV of France. The names of Berowne and his fellow attendant lords, Dumaine and Longaville, echo those of commanders on opposite sides of the war, the Ducs de Biron, De Mayenn and De Longueville.

The salon sophistication of *Love's Labour's Lost* makes it feel like the beating heart of a corpus of comedies germinating throughout Shakespeare's sojourn with Southampton, written as light relief from the technical complexities of the Sonnets and narrative poems. It is tempting to see his (or his patron's) exasperation with the opposite sex reflected in Petruchio's with Katharina in *The Taming of the Shrew* — even to cite Petruchio's eventual triumph over adversity as evidence that *The Shrew* is the mysteriously missing *Love's Labour's Won*, a title listed among Shakespeare's comedies by his contemporary Francis Meres in

1598 but conspicuous by its absence from the First Folio. Meres does not mention *The Shrew*, whose genesis is further complicated by the existence of a distinctly inferior play called *The Taming of a Shrew*, which saw print in 1594 'as it was sundry times acted by the Right Honourable the Earl of Pembroke his servants'; if a 'memorial reconstruction', for it is too weak to be a pirated text or corrupt quarto of any Shakespearean original, this was the work of actors with very bad memories indeed.

Onstage, in recent years, some of these early comedies have fared less well in their own right — antique, mothballed specimens accorded merely ex-officio reverence — than as pirated libretti for twentieth-century musicals. As *The Comedy of Errors* spawned Rogers and Hart's *The Boys from Syracuse*, so *The Taming of the Shrew* inspired Cole Porter's *Kiss Me Kate*. But even that now seems a quaint period-piece, unacceptable to millennial sensibilities. Shakespeare's play can be performed as a pre-feminist slice of male chauvinist propaganda, or a subtler Elizabethan take on the battle of the sexes; but it is undeniable that women are again demeaned, indeed man-handled, to the point where *The Shrew* has become a difficult work to stage successfully at the turn of the twenty-first century.

SHYLOCK: 'IS THAT THE LAW?',
FROM 'THE MERCHANT OF VENICE', 1597.
ETCHING BY ROBERT DUDLEY.

Twin masters with twin servants belong to an Italian *commedia dell'arte* tradition which flourished in the seventeenth century but stretched back long before — just as the termagant or shrewish wife had been a staple constituent of stage comedy since Plautus and Terence, via Chaucer to the Mystery Plays, where the nagging Mrs Noah was always causing trouble by refusing to abandon her fellow-gossips to board the Ark even as the Flood threatened to overwhelm the earth. Although, as always, a significant advance on its originals, using an age-old theme for a more profound exploration of their respective rights and needs of the sexes, *The Shrew* is closer to farce than the later, mature Shakespeare comedies, as indeed is *The Comedy of Errors*. Both already display masterly stagecraft, a vivid sense of theatre, and a lightness of comic touch; but both seem the product of a less sophisticated, perhaps less battle-scarred mind than *Love's Labour's Lost*. Because of the haze surrounding the dates of their composition – all that can be said with any confidence is that all three had been written by 1594 – each has rivalled the *Henry VI* trilogy, through the centuries, as candidates for the distinction of being Shakespeare's first solo work for the stage.

The first recorded performance of *The Comedy of Errors* – at 1,777 lines the shortest of all Shakespeare's plays, and yet one of the busiest – was at Gray's Inn on 28 December 1594. But its many stylistic links with narrative poems suggest that it must again have been written during Shakespeare's retreat from the plague in the Southampton household – less as a satire on domestic events, like its contemporary comedies, than a dazzling display of what the house poet could do with his Roman sources. Drawing on two plays of Plautus, *Menaechmi* and *Amphitruo*, Shakespeare made life difficult for himself by adding a second set of twins, and involving a wife rather than a courtesan in apparent infidelity.

Beneath its Keystone Cops surface, for all the dexterity of its plotting, *The Comedy of Errors* again sees Shakespeare exploring themes which would haunt his later work, from witchcraft and sorcery to the breakdown of social order, and the search for self complicated by awareness of parallel selves. Even at this early stage of his dramatic career, Shakespeare was also developing the notion that, to carry conviction, happy endings must be won from 'a serious confrontation with mortality, violence, and time.' As the twentieth century has seen other disciplines hijack Shakespeare studies for their own ends, American psychoanalysis has even divined in *The Comedy of Errors* the poet's expression of 'an unconscious desire for incest with his mother.'

Be this as it may, the 'Dark Lady' seems to have been but one of several shrewish London women who put Shakespeare through spasms of sexual jealousy so agonising as to wring from him, a decade and more later, graphic portrayals of the 'green-eyed monster' (in each case unwarranted) in *Othello* and *The Winter's Tale*. From the strength of feeling he also devoted to another, closely allied sexual topic, it seems equally likely that during these years away from his

(OPPOSITE)
ELIZABETH VERNON,
COUNTESS OF
SOUTHAMPTON, C.1605.
UNKNOWN ARTIST.

wife and children in Stratford the thirty-year-old poet was rewarded for his adventures in London with a bout or two of the clap (gonorrhoea). In 1594, amid the sexual antics of the Southampton household, Shakespeare was portrayed as a poet with the clap in yet another anonymous satire at his expense, *Willobie his Avisa*, or *The True Picture of a Modest Maid, and of a Chaste and Constant Wife* entered in Stationers Register on 3 September.

The same was said of his patron, Southampton, already living dangerously, by hitching his star to that of the reckless Essex, and underestimating Elizabeth's self-imposed mission as defender of the faith invented by her father. To make matters worse, *Willobie* could further be seen as a sustained satire on Southampton's illicit pursuit of the Queen's maid of honour, Elizabeth Vernon, while continuing to reject Lady Elizabeth de Vere, the potential bride for whom his guardian, Lord Burghley, had won royal approval.

(PAGES 142–143)
FALSTAFF WITH RECRUITS
AT JUSTICE SHALLOW'S,
FROM '2 HENRY IV'.
PAINTING BY
JAMES DURNO, C.1745–95.

AUTOLYCUS, FROM 'THE WINTER'S TALE', C.1610.
COLOUR LITHOGRAPH AFTER A DRAWING BY JOHN GILBERT,
1817–97.

So Elizabeth would have been far from amused by the suggestion that the earl had, in the course of all this misbehaviour, contracted a venereal disease.

If both Shakespeare and Southampton had both paid so dearly for their sexual pleasure, who was the guilty female party? Enter, again, the Dark Lady of the Sonnets, variously identified by scholars through the ages as any or all of the above. Whatever the true identity of this Elizabethan *femme fatale*, she appears not just to have put Shakespeare through the miseries of the clap, but to have lost him his patron. Between them, by the look of it, *Willobie* and the Dark Lady proved too much for Southampton, who chose this moment to break off professional – if not yet personal – relations with Shakespeare.

But this poet, like any force of nature, had a lifelong talent for making his own luck. Just as he would have been wondering where next to turn for money, the plague at last abated sufficiently for the theatres to reopen.

'YOUNG MAN
AMONG ROSES', C.1587.
PAINTING BY NICHOLAS
HILLIARD, 1547–1619.

To the Reader.

This Figure, that thou here seeſt put,
It vvas for gentle Shakeſpeare cut;
VVherein ... ſtrife
VVith N... the life :
O, could he ... his VVit
As well i... n hit
His Face ; t... en ſurpaſſe
All, that vv... Braſſe.
But, ſince he cannot, Reader, looke
Not on his Picture, but his Booke.

B. I.

VI
THE LORD CHAMBERLAIN'S MAN
1594–1599

Romeo and Juliet, Shakespeare's
first new work for the
Lord Chamberlain's Men
to stage in the reopened theatres,
was his most candid nod yet to
the box-office, and nothing less than
the first romantic tragedy ever to
be written.

As he parted company with one patron, so another returned from the past — albeit inadvertently — to his rescue. It was during Shakespeare's time in the service of Southampton that his Lancashire employers of so long ago, the recusant Hesketh family, took an even bolder stand against the heirless Virgin Queen, with disastrous consequences for them but a happier ending for Shakespeare.

The playwright had maintained his Lancashire connections through his professional dealings with the players of the Earl of Derby, otherwise known as Lord Strange's Servants. What began life as a private troupe for occasional in-house entertainments had become one of the handful of leading London-based companies, mirroring Shakespeare's progress from hired hand to leading player, by the time it was inherited by Derby's heir Ferdinando, Lord Strange, on his father's death in September 1593. But now, barely six months after inheriting his father's title, Ferdinando himself was dead at the age of only thirty-five.

Conspiracy theorists continue to doubt the modern view that the new earl died of natural causes on 16 April 1594, preferring to suspect foul play following his betrayal of Richard Hesketh, the recusant son of Lancashire executed for his role in the papist plot to make Derby king. Whatever the truth, Derby's (or Strange's) players were already in some disarray at the time of their patron's death, thanks to the prolonged closure of the London theatres. Back in business, they now regrouped under the patronage of Henry Carey, first Baron Hunsdon, Lord Chamberlain to the Queen, and Her Majesty's closest intimate. With Richard Burbage at its helm, along with his

GREENWICH PALACE
FROM THE NORTH BANK
OF THE THAMES.
DRAWING BY
ANTHONY VAN
WYNGAERDE, 1594.

(PAGE 146)
BENJAMIN JONSON.
PAINTING BY ABRAHAM
VAN BLYENBERCH,
FL.1617–22.
(OPPOSITE)
PORTRAIT OF
QUEEN ELIZABETH I,
1533–1603.
IN THE MANNER OF
NICHOLAS HILLIARD,
1547–1619.

ANN̄ᵒ DÑI 1581,   ÆTATIS SVÆ 44,

Sʳ Iohn Hawkins,

friends Will Shakespeare and Will Kemp, the new troupe proudly took the name of the Lord Chamberlain's Men.

On 8 October 1594 Hunsdon formally requested the Lord Mayor of London to permit his 'new' company of players to return to the stage after their long absence, with a series of performances at the Cross Key inn in Gracious Street. Just as *Willobie* and the Dark Lady saw him estranged from Southampton – if only, as it transpired, briefly – a no doubt relieved Shakespeare found himself back in gainful employment, required to abandon his immortal longings in the shape of narrative poetry to return to the production of a steady stream of new plays.

Henslowe's diary records that Hunsdon's company had briefly performed that June at Newington Butts; now, over Christmas, they played twice at court. The accounts of the Treasurer of the Queen's Chamber dated 15 March 1595 cite William Shakespeare as joint payee, with Richard Burbage and William Kempe ('servants to the Lord Chamberlain') for performances before the Queen at her palace at Greenwich on 26 and 27 December 1594. The following night saw them perform *The Comedy of Errors* for the Christmas 'law-revels' at Gray's Inn – an evening of such 'disordered tumult and crowd', by one account, that 'it was ever afterwards called "The Night of Errors".'

Shakespeare had now joined the theatrical company with which he would remain, throughout its changing guises, for the rest of his acting and writing life. Just as his income from Southampton dried up, it was the actor-playwright's good fortune that Burbage co-opted him and Kemp on to the management team of what soon became the pre-eminent stage troupe of the day, eventually to pass under royal patronage. The house dramatist and bit-part actor was also shrewd enough to become a shareholder in the Lord Chamberlain's Men. As actor, *ad hoc* director, shareholder and above all 'ordinary poet' of the company, thirty-year-old William Shakespeare was already, in the words of one twentieth-century authority, 'the most complete man of the theatre of his time'. Few in any age, observes another, have served the stage so variously: 'not Racine or Ibsen or Shaw; only Molière, besides Shakespeare, among playwrights of world stature.'

Newly installed in lodgings in St Helen's, Bishopsgate, as close to the

(OPPOSITE)
SIR JOHN HAWKINS,
1532–95.
ENGLISH SCHOOL
SIXTEENTH CENTURY.
PAINTING BY JOHANN
HEINRICH FÜSSLI,
1744–1825.

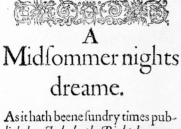

A Midfommer nights dreame.

As it hath beene fundry times pub-
lickely acted, by the Right honourable, the Lord Chamberlaine his
feruants.

Written by William Shakespeare.

¶ Imprinted at London, for *Thomas Fisher*, and are to
be soulde at his shoppe, at the Signe of the White Hart,
in *Fleetestreete.* 1600.

TITLE PAGE OF THE
FIRST QUARTO OF
'A MIDSOMMER NIGHT'S DREAME',
1600.

stews of Clerkenwell as the theatres of Shoreditch, Shakespeare would now have less time (and, perhaps, energy) to expend his spirit in a waste of shame. As his reconstituted colleagues gratefully staged the plays he had written during their exile from London, with the clown Kemp relishing the role of Costard in *Love's Labour's Lost*, the prolific house dramatist was already required to get to work on more. Soon he would exorcise the demons of the clap with a tragically chaste love story, *Romeo and Juliet*. But first there was a non-fictional marriage to celebrate, which called for a stylish *pièce d'occasion*. Shakespeare may well have begun work on *A Midsummer Night's Dream* while still a member of Southampton's household. As resident poet, he would have been required to come up with an entertainment to mark the marriage of the earl's mother, the dowager countess Mary, to the Treasurer of the Queen's Chamber, Sir Thomas Heneage, on 2 May 1594.

Had the noble earl occasionally complained to Shakespeare about his mother's longevity, postponing his inheritance of his birthright? As a financial beneficiary of both, the poet would have taken as close an interest as he did in those maternal pressures on the young earl to marry — already explored in the Sonnets and *Love's Labour's Lost*, now reflected in the chaotic pairings of *A Midsummer Night's Dream*, all caused (as in *Romeo and Juliet*) by a parent's attempt to foist an unwelcome match on an offspring in love elsewhere. The unusually high number of female parts in the play, no doubt stretching the abilities of the available boy actors, may have constituted some gentle ribbing by the poet of his patron. If they had fallen out over the Dark Lady, or indeed any other female of the night, the rift between them was short-lived, and more professional than personal, allowing Shakespeare to gratify his noble friend with some risqué jokes at his unwitting mother's expense.

One measure of the gulf between Shakespeare and his sources is that some of the wilfully clumsy lines given to Bottom as Pyramus, in the burlesque of the play-within-the-play, were written as straightforward speeches in such obscure originals as Preston's *Cambises* (1561) and *Appius and Virginia* (1564). As

(OPPOSITE)
TITANIA IN THE GRIP
OF HER FANTASTIC
DELUSION, FROM
'A MIDSUMMER
NIGHT'S DREAM'.
PAINTING BY
RUDOLF CARL HUBER
1839–96.

Bottom-turned-Pyramus, Burbage would have relished the chance to parody Ned Alleyn's acting style, all swagger and bombast, with no hint or subtlety or humour – a mode of performance and indeed writing which Shakespeare and the Lord Chamberlain's Men were swiftly consigning to a bygone age.

From a complex celebration of marriage in the abstract to a brutally realistic portrayal of young love thwarted: *Romeo and Juliet*, Shakespeare's first new work for the Lord Chamberlain's Men to stage in the reopened theatres, his most candid nod yet to the box-office, and nothing less than the first romantic tragedy ever to be written. Tracing its lineage back through all the great love pairings of literature, from Ovid's Pyramus and Thisbe to Chaucer's Troilus and Criseyde, the play may again have bowed to Southampton in portraying the disastrous consequences of misplaced parental pressure in the matter of marriage; and it was again Southampton's circle which provided the context the poet needed to make his reworking of an age-old theme peculiarly Shakespearean.

WOODCUT OF THE STORY OF
PYRAMUS AND THISBE.
ITALIAN SCHOOL, SIXTEENTH CENTURY.

The poet's last months in the earl's employ saw the climax of a dispute between friends and neighbours of Southampton's, the Danvers and the Longs, which dated as far back as the Wars of the Roses. Like all such feuds, it ebbed and flowed in intensity, reaching an especially violent climax early in 1594. So Shakespeare had vivid, first-hand experience of such mindless vendettas, prone to fatal consequences, as that symbolised by the Italian families of Montecchi and Capelletti (names to be found in Dante's *Purgatorio*). He was already familiar with Arthur Brooke's 1562 poem 'The Tragicall Historye of Romeus and Iuilet', an English amalgam of two centuries of European folkloric tradition, on which he had drawn for *The Two Gentlemen of Verona*. In a prefatory Address to the Reader, the dull, moralistic Brooke stressed the role of fate in the downfall of his lovers; and it is this same Senecan element of chance in Shakespeare's adaptation, depriving his star-crossed lovers of responsibility for

(OPPOSITE)
CAPULET'S GARDEN, FROM
'ROMEO AND JULIET'.
PAINTING BY
CHARLES EDOUARD
EDMOND DELORT,
1841–95.

To Shakespeare, who was privy to all this, it must have seemed that Her Majesty's Lord High Treasurer had been evaluating Lady Elizabeth's frustrated affections as if they were merely 'precious metal'. Coinciding as it did with a notorious scandal at court, resulting in a trial and execution which had all London agog, the episode emboldened him to venture into uncharted territory, writing Burbage his most powerful part yet as he followed one fable with another — a parable exploring his lifelong ambivalence about money, with especial reference to the usury which had so haunted his stricken father.

It was supposedly their practice of usury — lending money for interest, forbidden to Christians under canon if not secular law — which had caused Edward I to expel all Jewish residents from English soil in 1290. Three hundred years later, the ban was still technically in force; but a thin line of a few hundred Jews were to be found living in Elizabethan London, tolerated on the assumption that they disguised their religion, and kept any moneylending well out of sight of the law. By professing Christianity, some even

'LOPEZ COMPOUNDING TO POYSON THE QUEENE'.
ENGRAVING FROM 'A THANKFUL DEMONSTRANCE OF
GOD'S MERCY' BY G. CARLTON, 1627.

managed to achieve acceptance in the highest circles, notably a Portuguese-born Jewish doctor named Roderigo Lopez, who rose to become physician to the Earl of Leicester, and then to the Queen herself.

Once a useful spy for Sir Francis Walsingham's secret service, Lopez was dangerously slow to transfer his loyalties to the Earl of Essex after Walsingham's death in 1590. On a trumped-up accusation of political intrigue, supposedly on behalf of a pretender to the Portuguese throne then exiled in London, Essex accused the Queen's doctor of trying to poison her. There were scant grounds for the charge, based on evidence invented by Essex and supposedly extracted by torture, but Lopez was tried for treason in February 1594 and executed at Tyburn on 7 June — castrated, hung, cut down while still alive,

disembowelled and quartered in front of a baying crowd that might just have included an inquisitive (if appalled) Shakespeare, whose friend and former patron, Southampton, was one of Essex's most devoted followers.

Hitherto dormant in Elizabethan England, anti-Jewish sentiment was inflamed by the Lopez case, largely at Essex's orchestration. It was in the ambitious earl's interests to lend notoriety to the scandal he had sponsored, to which end he encouraged revivals of Marlowe's *The Jew of Malta* (1589), performed on no fewer than fifteen occasions during the period of the Jewish doctor's trial and execution. Sensing a box-office opportunity, Shakespeare too soon set about writing a 'play of the hour', *The Merchant of Venice*, in which there is at least one direct reference to the Lopez case.

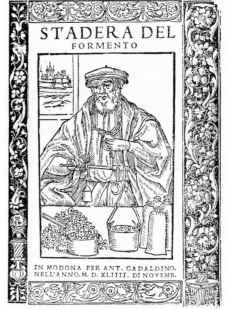

If Shakespeare's primary debt was to *The Jew of Malta*, it is a typical advance to differentiate his Shylock so utterly from Marlowe's Barabas — a caricature of a ruthless Machiavel, whose indiscriminate slaughter for no more than financial gain takes in an entire nunnery. Where Marlowe merely reflected stereotypical Elizabethan attitudes to Jews, seen in the popular imagination almost as 'mythical beasts: strange, evil beings who had once crucified Christ and might be expected to persevere in anti-Christian activities', Shakespeare painted a more profound portrait of racism and religious prejudices reeking of contemporary resonance for every subsequent era, not least our own.

UNATTRIBUTED ENGRAVING OF MERCHANT COUNTING MONEY-LENDING PROFITS.

There is no doubt that Shakespeare's father, and probably the poet himself, developed a sideline as a money-lender, despite stern Tudor laws. Among documents only recently discovered are Exchequer transactions adding to John Shakespeare's track-record in usury, officially deemed 'a vice most odious and detestable'. In 1570 John 'Shappere alias Shakespeare' of 'Stratford upon Haven' was fined 40 shillings for charging £20 interest on an £80 loan to one John Musshem of Walton D'Eiville. Shakespeare's father had been reported to the authorities by one of their most persistent informants, James Langrake of Whittlebury, Northamptonshire, who would name him again, more than once,

(OPPOSITE)
DATCHET MEAD FROM 'THE MERRY WIVES OF WINDSOR'.
PAINTING BY JOHN S. CLIFTON, FL.1848–69.

for illegal transactions in wool. Whatever angst these public accusations and court proceedings caused Shakespeare's father seems to have made a lasting impression on his schoolboy son. For all his own practice of arranging loans, a distaste for the phenomenon of money, and all the trouble it can engender, would haunt much of his subsequent work, reaching a crescendo in *Timon of Athens*.

The summer of 1595 saw food riots on the streets of London. Eggs flew and butter smeared the pavements in protest at sudden price increases. A poor harvest had coincided with an outbreak of cattle disease, and the market traders were quick to capitalise. Martial law was proclaimed, rioters summarily executed on Tower Hill, and the theatres – potential hotbeds of seditious assembly – closed down for two months.

There are those who think the capitalist in Shakespeare saw him seize the moment, like many Londoners with sufficient funds, to cash in on the misfortune of others by buying grain cheap and selling it dear. Whatever his feelings about the evils wrought by money, the poet was never averse to accumulating it. This time the metaphors could wait – a dozen years, as it transpired, before surfacing as the fable of the belly told a restive crowd in Coriolanus' Rome. For now, there were other political developments to occupy his mind, challenge his powers of survival in smart society, and of course feed his work.

Since the Lopez affair, Essex had been out of favour at court. Shakespeare himself may have found much to deplore in his and Southampton's glee at the Portuguese Jew's unjust downfall; more important, to the career prospects of these noblemen, Elizabeth herself had been unamused by their hounding of her 'little ape'. In vain had even the monarch, reluctant to believe the evidence against Lopez, attempted to intervene in the legal process; now her only solace was to shun Essex, once her conspicuous favourite. As a second Spanish armada gathered, at a time when her leading admirals Drake and Hawkins were far distant on a voyage from which they would not return, the Catholic enemy appeared ready to take advantage of the Queen's continuing failure to name an heir. In truth she already had the Protestant King James VI of Scotland in mind, and was embarked on a long

(OPPOSITE)
SIR FRANCIS DRAKE,
C.1580.
UNKNOWN ARTIST.

correspondence to test his mettle; but she kept her own counsel in the matter, lest Catholic assassins took it into their own impetuous hands.

Was it Shakespeare himself who chose this moment to return to historical drama, specifically a 'prequel' to his *Henry VI–Richard III* cycle, showing the origins of the primal curse on the House of Bolingbroke: the deposition and murder of Richard II by his cousin, Henry IV? Or was it at the suggestion of Southampton, on a hint from Essex, that he decided to tackle the touchy theme of a nation labouring under weak leadership, so weak as to justify the intervention of a heroic usurper? There were lessons still for the Tudors to learn from the origins of the Wars of the Roses, and Shakespeare set out to dramatise them in his portrayal of Richard II. The deposition scene, tactfully omitted when the play was published two years later, and again when it was twice republished during Elizabeth's lifetime, would predictably return to cause trouble to all concerned. In the meantime, Shakespeare went to some pains to distance his subject-matter from too much topical relevance.

The historical Richard II, son of the Black Prince and last of the Angevins, was a weak, unjust and extravagant ruler. He was only fourteen when the Peasants' Revolt was put down with great severity, but it was his later attempt to abandon parliamentary government which proved his rapid undoing. Drawing on Holinshed's *Chronicles* (first published in 1577, revised and enlarged in 1587) and John Foxe's *Book of Martyrs* (1563), Shakespeare lent the King an introspective moral ambiguity which flattered him, rendering him quite distinct from the flamboyance of his hunch-backed successor, last of the Lancastrian line.

In intensely lyrical verse, Shakespeare embodies the old order in the nostalgic patriotism of John of Gaunt, whose imperious warnings the King ignores, and whose properties he confiscates after his death, inflaming his exiled son Henry Bolingbroke to return to England in search of justice. As the balance of power shifts, so do the audience's sympathies, with Richard eloquently lamenting the loss of his throne,

BURNING AT THE STAKE. ILLUSTRATION FROM 'ACTES AND MONUMENTS' (BETTER KNOWN AS THE 'BOOK OF MARTYRS') BY JOHN FOXE, 1563.

and achieving a degree of self-knowledge in a fine soliloquy before his murder in jail at the hands of Piers Exton. Richard dies insisting, significantly to Shakespeare's audience, that he was still the rightful monarch. Henry denies responsibility for Richard's death, but takes himself off on a guilt-ridden pilgrimage to the Holy Land, sowing the seeds of the Wars of the Roses with an inevitability echoing the scale and power of Aeschylus' *Oresteia*.

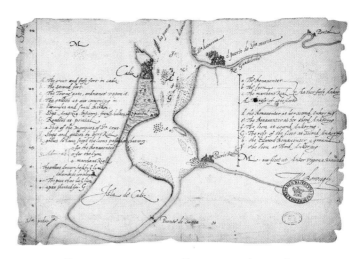

PLAN OF THE ATTACK ON CADIZ ON 29 APRIL 1587.
PAINTING BY WILLIAM BOROUGH, 1537–99.

In Richard's ornate wordplay, sudden mood-swings and regal tantrums, another virtuoso role was created by Shakespeare for Burbage. In John of Gaunt's famous deathbed speech – 'This precious stone set in a silver sea ... This blessed plot, this earth, this realm, this England' – he gave the groundlings the jingoistic morale boost they craved at a time of apparent danger from Spain. Rarely does it seem clearer that these were far from being the poet's own sentiments; qualified, anyway, by his lament for a lost England, fallen on hard times, Gaunt's patriotic zeal prepares the way for the dramatist's cynicism when he came to chronicle subsequent events. As the Lord Chamberlain's Men staged four performances for the Queen at the end of 1595, the *Henry IV–V* trilogy was already taking shape in Shakespeare's mind.

First, he would reach further back in English history, and indeed his own stage career, to hand his colleagues more topical box-office fare by reworking one of the hardy annuals of the Queen's Men, *The Troublesome Reign of King John*. With Calais fallen to the papist Spaniards, France exulting in the discomfiture of the English, and a fleet despatched to Cadiz under the joint command of a rehabilitated Essex and the Lord Admiral, Lord Charles Howard, the punters were in a mood to hear the French roundly scorned and the Pope put in his place. The relish with which he demeans the papal emissary, Cardinal Pandulph, suggests that Shakespeare was by now abandoning the last vestiges of any religious belief, orthodox or otherwise; in the condemnation of organised religion implicit in *King John,* a greater work of poetry than of drama, can be traced the beginnings of the poet's increasingly nihilistic progress through *Troilus and Cressida* to the great tragedies.

But they still lay ten years off. And that summer of *King John,* that hot August of 1596, Shakespeare of the waning faith had good reason finally to forswear his Catholic God and rail against the cruelly arbitrary injustices of human life. If ever, throughout Shakespeare's twenty-five years in London, we can assume that he was back home in Stratford on a specific date, it would have been 11 August 1596 — to bury his son Hamnet, dead at the age of eleven.

Shakespeare was only thirty-two, but his wife Anne was already forty, past the age to consider bearing him more children. Beyond the personal grief which now becomes a recurring strain in his work, through *Hamlet* and beyond, Shakespeare had been robbed of a direct line of descent. That he cared about this seems evident from the fact that he had only recently reapplied, perhaps to please his father as much as to gratify his own *amour propre,* for the coat of arms denied John Shakespeare back in 1569. William's brothers Gilbert, Richard and Edmund were now thirty, twenty-two and sixteen respectively; but all four of them would be dead, with no surviving male issue, within fifteen years of their father. There was now no Fleance to stretch the Shakespeare line to the crack of doom. Now it would die just twenty years later with its most famous son.

As befits a born poet, Shakespeare would grieve for his son throughout his remaining work. The shade of young Hamnet would stalk his father's lines for many a play to come. At the time, ironically, this worst year of Shakespeare's life coincided with a sudden upswing in his worldly fortunes; as his wealth increased to the point where he could consider buying a substantial property, the College of Arms deigned to grant his family the coat of arms denied his father nearly thirty years earlier. The Shakespeare family's somewhat half-hearted new motto seemed almost to acknowledge its surprise at the success of this second application: *Non Sanz Droict,* 'not without right' (later satirised by Ben Jonson as 'not without mustard').

With his father approaching seventy, a great age for the day, Shakespeare

(OPPOSITE)
JOHN OF GAUNT,
DUKE OF LANCASTER,
1340–99, 4TH SON OF
EDWARD III.
UNKNOWN ARTIST.

HON: SOIT: QVI: MAL: Y: PENSE

EDVARDI TERTII REX
CASTELLÆ: ET LEGION
DVX LANCASTRIÆ
CONSTABVLARIVS CAS
DE QVEENSBOVRG: COV
TO OCTOBRIS ANNO
REGNI ELIW TERTII AN
GLIÆ 50. FRANCIÆ 3

touchingly sought to exorcise his fall from civic grace by more than merely a grant of arms and the status of gentleman. Now his loyal son, deprived of his own, saw to it that the Shakespeares could be regarded as Stratford's ex-officio first family, owners of the finest residence in town – a fit setting, in due course, for his retirement.

Since the mid-1590s Shakespeare had been a householder in London, in the St Helen's parish of Bishopsgate ward, as we know from the inclusion of his name among property tax defaulters listed by the Exchequer Office in November 1597 and October 1598. As family dramas saw him journeying to and from Stratford with unusual frequency, he also took a fancy to the idea of buying New Place, the biggest house in Stratford, built in the 1490s by that same Clopton who had become Lord Mayor of London, giving his name to the bridge across the Avon where all journeys to the capital commenced.

New Place was sold to the newly genteel actor-playwright by William Underhill, son of a prosperous lawyer-landowner who had restored the property from the state of 'great ruine and decay' in which he himself had purchased it thirty years earlier. With its sixty-foot frontage, ten rooms, two gardens, two orchards and two barns, this 'grete house' was a bargain at £60 – too much so, perhaps, in the view of Underhill's son, who poisoned his father two months later, for which he was duly hanged in Warwick.

Leaving Anne and his daughters at last installed in a home of their own – and a handsome one at that, just around the corner from his parents in Henley Street – Shakespeare returned to London to find the backdrop of his professional life fast changing. The Queen had appointed a new Lord Chamberlain – another Lord Hunsdon, happily enough, son of the late patron of Shakespeare's troupe of players – while the fortunes of his other friend and former patron, Southampton, were fluctuating dangerously with those of the Earl of Essex.

The previous August, the same month as Hamnet's death, Essex had returned in triumph from the fall of Cadiz – heartening revenge, to public

PORTRAIT OF JOHN OF GAUNT,
DUKE OF LANCASTER, 1340–99
FROM ILLUMINATED MANUSCRIPT.

(OPPOSITE)
LORD CHARLES
HOWARD.
PAINTING BY
DANIEL MYTENS.

opinion, for the loss of Calais. But Southampton was not, for once, at the ambitious earl's side as he rode in triumph through the streets of London. The Queen had upset him by keeping him back from the expedition, suspicious about his flirtation with her lady-in-waiting, Elizabeth Vernon. Before long, she would be proved right when Elizabeth became pregnant by Southampton. Like his poet-friend, the earl did the honourable thing by Mistress Vernon, marrying her in a secret ceremony in Paris. On their return, the Queen signalled her extreme displeasure by clapping them both in jail.

To the Reader.

This Figure, that thou here seeft put,
It was for gentle Shakespeare cut;
Wherein the Graver had a strife
VVith Nature, to out-doo the life :
O, could he but have dravvne his VVit
As well in Brasse, as he hath hit
His Face ; the Print vvould then surpasse
All, that vvas ever vvrit in Brasse.
But, since he cannot, Reader, looke
Not on his Picture, but his Booke.
B. I.

BEN JONSON'S DEDICATION TO SHAKESPEARE
IN THE 1ST FOLIO EDITION OF HIS WORK, 1623.

Shakespeare had his own distractions during this difficult period, with the arrival on the theatrical scene of a rival talent in the shape of Ben Jonson, eight years his junior, yet far more gifted than any literary opposition he had yet encountered. But before long he and Shakespeare had become friends. On the one hand, Jonson was an unlikely convert to Catholicism (until 1610, when he drank off the entire Communion chalice to mark his return to the Anglican church); on the other he had killed a man, for which his thumb was branded with a T for Tyburn. But what was that, in these unruly times, to Shakespeare? It was he who brought Jonson over to the Lord Chamberlain's company, who the following year gave the first performances of Jonson's *Every Man in His Humour*, with Shakespeare himself in the role of the elder Kno'well. When Jonson published his *Collected Works* in 1616, the year of Shakespeare's death, he accorded his friend pride of place among the 'principal comedians' in the cast list on the title page.

It was typical of Shakespeare's 'humanity and good nature', in Rowe's words, that he lent a helping hand to a rival then 'altogether unknown to the world'. Ever after, Rowe continues, the two writers were 'professed friends, though I don't know whether the other [Jonson] ever made him [Shakespeare] an equal return of gentleness and sincerity'. Longer hindsight knows better.

Shakespeare and Jonson show every sign of having remained firm friends until Shakespeare's death, after which Jonson did him due credit in a series of verse tributes, notably that adorning the frontispiece to the First Folio of the Collected Plays, published in 1623.

In *Richard II*, chronologically the first part of the mightiest history cycle ever written for the stage, Shakespeare had gone to some pains (often distorting the historical facts) to reassert the prevailing belief that the English monarch was chosen by God. He or she was not on the throne by virtue of talent, prestige or prowess, but as 'God's substitute, His deputy anointed in His right'. As Elizabeth continued to resist increasing demands to name an heir, and so to face potential threats from Catholic usurpers, the playwright's preoccupation with comparatively recent English history was understandable. Amid the uneasy peace of the late 1590s, it seemed timely to reassert the received wisdom that usurpers would come to no good, even if fate took a few generations to catch up with them.

It had taken him three plays to cover the long, tortuous reign of Henry VI, one to capture the short, brutish one of Richard III. All this time, it seems, he had longed to square the circle by returning to the roots of all that evil, prefacing a two-part panorama of the usurper Henry Bolingbroke with his seizure of Richard II's throne, and following it with the short but glorious reign of his blameless son Henry V. He had already chronicled England's subsequent decline into civil war, the logical consequence of Henry Bolingbroke's original sin in 1399. Not until Richard III's death at Bosworth would Henry's crime finally be expiated, and the natural order restored.

With the completion of this mighty history cycle – eight plays covering five reigns from 1377 to 1485 – Shakespeare sought to demonstrate the consequences of interfering with the divine order not merely as they affected the principal players, but also the hapless subjects whose lives are disrupted, often ended by decades of disorder and civil strife. Never more than in the two parts of *Henry IV* did he so vividly depict the suffering of the common man as the pawn of warring power-brokers. If Henry himself can never, like Macbeth, live to enjoy the throne he played so foully for – 'Uneasy lies the head that wears

a crown' — so his offence affects the rest of the nation, which pays an equally heavy price.

As the plays oscillate between the court and its subjects, from the field to the inn, Shakespeare's humour breaks through for the first time in his history plays. In the process he created one of his most-loved roles, second only to Hamlet among characters in whom his readers see reflections of themselves. Sir John Falstaff was originally called Sir John Oldcastle, a name he revived from a play dating back to his days with the Queen's Men, *The Famous Victories of Henry V*. But recent history contained a real Sir John Oldcastle, a Lollard martyr hanged and burned in St Giles's Fields in 1417, during Henry V's reign, for denouncing the Pope as the Antichrist. This Oldcastle was also Lord Cobham, a title still worn with pride by his lineal descendant William Brooke, a Privy Councillor and Lord Chamberlain. The powerful Lord Cobham lodged protests in high places, including the office of the Master of the Revels, to the point where Shakespeare felt obliged to change the name to that of the cowardly character already glimpsed in the first scene of his *I Henry VI*.

Elizabeth I must have been aware of the controversy; indeed, according to Rowe, it was the Queen herself who 'was pleas'd to command' Shakespeare to 'alter' the name. Nonetheless, she was sufficiently enamoured of the character of the indomitable old knight to commission a sequel. Elizabeth was 'so well pleased with the admirable character of Falstaff', according to a tradition begun in 1705 by Charles Gildon, the minor writer satirised by Pope in *The Dunciad*, 'that she commanded [Shakespeare] to continue it for one play more, and to show him in love'. We have the word of the serious-minded and responsible playwright John Dennis that *The Merry Wives of Windsor* was written in ten days, two weeks at most, which suggests that Shakespeare was none too pleased to be royally diverted from his second historical tetralogy.

Nor did he make, by his standards, much effort. His least funny comedy was a rush job, as much to pay tribute to his company's patron as to gratify the Queen's desire to see Falstaff 'in love' (which, in fact, we *don't* see). Elizabeth, ever fonder of Hunsdon, had now made him a Knight of the Order of the Garter, whose annual feast was held in the Whitehall Palace on St George's Day, 23 April 1597. Both monarch and Lord Chamberlain would have been

(OPPOSITE)
ROBERT DEVEREUX,
2ND EARL OF ESSEX,
C.1587.
PAINTING BY
NICHOLAS HILLIARD,
1547–1619.

delighted by Shakespeare's courteous references to the Garter knights — their stalls in the chapel at Windsor, their crests, even their motto, *Honi soit qui mal y pense* — at the end of his little entertainment, repeated that summer to mark Hunsdon's installation at Windsor. Once again, Shakespeare seems to have pleased his monarch. The title page of the 1602 quarto specifies that *The Merry Wives* had oft been acted 'before Her Majesty'.

But the expansive character of Falstaff was demeaned by mere pantomime lechery. Without his brilliant wit, his sparkling repartee, his literary allusions, he was a mere shadow of the multi-faceted obstacle Shakespeare had deliberately placed in Hal's path to his father's throne. If Falstaff's creator had any doubts about killing him off before proceeding to *Henry V*, and the climax of his mighty history cycle, *Merry Wives* must have staunched them. To burnish his portrait of prodigal-son-turned-glorious king, and to gratify the groundlings' vision of *Henry V*, Falstaff had to go. The second part of *King Henry IV* may be less Sir John's play than the first, climaxing in his crushing rejection by the new king — 'I know thee not, old man' — but he is absent altogether from *Henry V*. The character had served his purpose. Yet even as the playwright moves on to less complex themes, vindicating the new Henry's rejection of his past, he diverts to pay Falstaff due homage with a noble death, in touching reported speech from his would-have-been wife, Mistress Quickly.

DEEDS OF TITLE OF THE
DUCHY OF LANCASTER, C.1402.
KING HENRY IV'S PORTRAIT APPEARS
IN THE ILLUMINATED INITIAL.

If the Queen was sitting up to Shakespeare, so was the theatregoing public. The second quartos of *Richard II* and *Richard III*, both published in 1598, marked the first time his name appeared on the title page as the author of any of his works, which had by now been appearing in print — in wholly random fashion, without his involvement or consent — for four years.

(OPPOSITE)
QUEEN ELIZABETH I
BEFORE PARLIAMENT,
1608.
PAINTING BY
ROBERT GLOVER.

By 1598 at least eight of Shakespeare's plays had appeared in print. That he had written more we know from another of that year's publications, *Palladis Tamia*, or *Wit's Treasury*, by Francis Meres, that tireless chronicler of the literary and theatrical scene. Meres's huge catalogue of literary witticisms, running to seven hundred octavo pages, showers praise on Shakespeare for 'mightily' enriching the English language, investing it in 'rare ornaments and resplendent habiliments'. Meres was the first, in print, to sense Shakespeare's true greatness, not hesitating to elevate this actor-writer above his contemporaries, hoisting him onto a par with the immortals.

But success and fame, then as now, come at a price. Neighbours will

(OPPOSITE)
HERMIA AND HELENA,
FROM 'A MIDSUMMER
NIGHT'S DREAM'.
PAINTING BY
JOSEPH SEVERN
1793–1879.

(BELOW)
PROCESSION OF THE
GARTER KNIGHTS.

always be neighbours. With this sudden renown following hard upon the heels of his *nouveau riche* purchase of New Place, it is scant surprise that the only surviving item of correspondence addressed to Shakespeare is a begging letter, written at this time by a Stratford friend visiting London. 'You shall friend me much in helping me out of all the debts I owe in London,' wrote Richard Quiney from the Bell inn in Carter Lane, near St Paul's, on 25 October 1598, asking his 'loving good friend and countryman Mr. Wm. Shackespere' for a loan of £30. Quiney was privy to his brother Adrian's hint to another mutual friend, Abraham Sturley, that Shakespeare might be 'willing to disburse some money' on land, property or other investments. According to his brother, Sturley told Quiney, 'our countryman Mr. Shaksper … thinketh it a very fit pattern to move him to deal in the matter of our tithes'.

There is no evidence that Shakespeare invested any money with Sturley, nor that he advanced Quiney that £30. The letter remained unsent; it was found among Quiney's papers after his death four years later. By then he was bailiff of Stratford again, mortally wounded while intervening in a drunken brawl involving some unsavoury associates of Shakespeare's brother Gilbert; in 1598

UNATTRIBUTED ENGRAVING OF VIEW OF
BLACKFRIARS STAIRS
AND SURROUNDING BUILDINGS, C.1660.

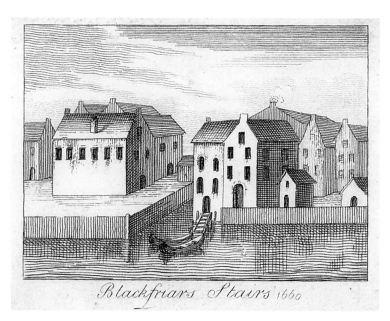

Blackfriars Stairs 1660

he was a city elder in London on Stratford business, petitioning the Privy Council for larger subventions to a town hard-hit by bad weather and two ruinous fires. It seems curious that he tried to sting Shakespeare on his own behalf, rather than Stratford's. Why was the letter not sent? Did Quiney think better of it? Or did he beard Shakespeare later that day at his lodgings, thinking a personal plea might prove more effective? Some biographers have assumed the poet generous (or crafty) enough to have made the loan, perhaps charging interest; others, citing Shakespeare's tight-fistedness, assert with equal confidence that Quiney returned home empty-handed.

One long-term worry may have made Shakespeare more than usually reluctant to part with cash just now, may indeed have had him feeling less prosperous than all other outward signs suggest. Throughout these last two years the Lord Chamberlain's Men had maintained their status as London's leading players against the dispiriting backdrop of an intractable legal crisis which threatened their very future. On 13 April 1597 James Burbage's twenty-one-year lease on the Theatre, the company's home since its foundation, had expired. For months he had been trying to negotiate a new lease with his absentee landlord, the recalcitrant Giles Alleyn, who was driving a very hard bargain. Burbage grew as desperate as his in-house players. He agreed to a vastly increased rent, from £14 to £24, and was even in the process of conceding Alleyn's eventual right to take possession of the building itself. Under the existing agreement Burbage owned the structure, Alleyn the land on which it stood. Now Alleyn inserted a clause asserting his right, after only five more years' tenancy, to convert the Theatre 'to some better use'. Burbage's patience snapped.

AN ELECTROTYPE OF THE ALABASTER EFFIGY OF HENRY IV IN CANTERBURY CATHEDRAL. UNKNOWN ELECTROTYPIST AFTER UNKNOWN ARTIST, C.1408–27.

Urgently he cast around for an alternative site, which he found in the disused refectory of the dissolved Blackfriars monastery, on the north bank of the Thames. Already it had been used by Lyly for genteel performances by his company of boy actors; but he too had fallen out with his landlord, leaving the run-down structure as the occasional venue for exhibitions of fencing. As part of a former monastery, though within the city walls, the building came under the aegis of the Crown, not the Lord Mayor and Council of London – a useful bonus which saw Burbage pledge the huge sum of £600 for the purchase of the structure, plus several hundred more for its conversion into a playhouse.

Just when the future again looked bright – with the intriguing promise for Shakespeare of writing plays for a wholly-covered, indoor playhouse – the

well-heeled residents of Blackfriars thwarted Burbage, with a successful protest to the Privy Council at the prospect of all the low life a playhouse would attract into their fashionable back yard. In the midst of it all, in January 1597, bowed down by months of pressure and anxiety, James Burbage dropped dead.

Robbed of their impresario, whose sons Richard and Cuthbert desperately reopened negotiations with Alleyn, the Lord Chamberlain's Men struggled on for eighteen months – through the expiry of the lease in April and into the next autumn, by which time the unscrupulous landlord knew he had them at his mercy. The company's only other available venue, the Curtain, was too run-down to offer the players a secure long-term future. With Richard Burbage playing the charmer, and poor Cuthbert quite miscast as the hard-headed businessman, the landlord slyly held out hope, while again making impossible demands – all of which Cuthbert felt obliged to concede, until Alleyn refused to accept the Burbage brothers as their own financial guarantors. Now he threatened to 'pull down' the Theatre, and 'to convert the wood and timber thereof to some better use'. In the meantime he retreated to his country seat, leaving his defeated tenants to lick their wounds. But something in the phrasing of this terrible threat, beyond the snide implications of the words 'some better use', gave the Burbages and their colleagues a wonderfully bright idea.

They may not have been able to hold on to the site of the Theatre, but at least they still owned the structure. On 28 December 1598 a conspiratorial group led by the Burbage brothers – and including, we can but hope, Shakespeare – convened in Shoreditch at dusk, with only the hours of darkness to carry out an ingenious plan. The widow Burbage is said to have 'looked on approvingly' as her sons supervised the dismantling of their late father's beloved Theatre.

The brothers' new financial partner William Smith was there, too, to see a team of a dozen workmen led by their chief carpenter, Peter Street, tenderly take the building down, plank by plank. The Burbages had found a new site across the river, in St Saviour's Parish, near the Rose. Thither, under cover of darkness, they proceeded to ferry the mortal remains of the Theatre – to reconstruct it over the next six months as a new playhouse, the finest yet built, to be called the Globe.

(OPPOSITE)
CORIOLANUS.
PAINTING BY
PUERRE JOSEPH CELESTIN
FRANCOIS, 1759–1851.

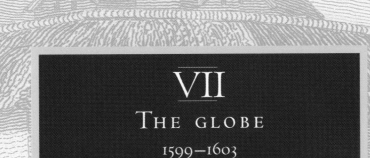

VII

THE GLOBE

1599—1603

The play most likely to have
opened the Globe in the summer of
1599 is *Henry V*, whose opening
Chorus contains an inaugural-sounding
reference to 'this wooden O',
within whose walls spectators are
asked to lend their imaginations
to 'piece out our imperfections with
your thoughts'.

On 21 September 1599, 'after dinner, about two o'clock', a Swiss tourist named Thomas Platter 'went with my party across the water; in the straw-thatched house we saw the tragedy of the first Emperor Julius Caesar, very pleasantly performed, with approximately fifteen characters; at the end of the play they danced together admirably and exceedingly gracefully, according to their custom, two in each group dressed in men's and two in women's apparel.'

The building of the Globe had taken the Burbages' carpenters all spring. But the theatre had opened several months before Platter's visit in September, probably as early as June. It is described as 'newly built' ('*de novo edificata*') on 16 May, in an inventory of the effects of the late Sir Thomas Brend, whose son Nicholas leased the site to William Shakespeare and others, by then already in occupation ('*in occupacione Willielmi Shakespeare et aliorum*'). In St Saviour's parish, on semi-cultivated land provocatively close to Henslowe's Rose, Shakespeare and the Burbages had overseen the swift rebirth of the Theatre's poor, bare planks as the most lavish, best-equipped playhouse in town, with a capacity of 2,500 to 3,000.

As soon as it opened it was doing booming business, and Shakespeare gloriously embarked on his most productive period, for the theatre which would play host to his greatest triumphs. As well as being house playwright, and bit-part actor, he was a shareholder in the Globe, as testified by records of the Court of Requests. Under a legal contract signed on 21 February 1599 Shakespeare owned a tenth of the Globe, as did his fellow actors John Heminges, Will Kemp, Augustine Phillips and Thomas Pope. Larger shares were held by landlord Brend and the Burbage brothers. Trustees included wealthy merchants named William Leveson and Thomas Savage of Rufford, Lancashire, that same village where the young Shakespeare had served in the Hesketh household.

At much the same time, as befits a man whose life

WATERCOLOUR OF
THE GLOBE THEATRE, SOUTHWARK.

(PAGE 182)
FRANCIS BACON,
VISCOUNT ST ALBAN,
C.1618.
PAINTING, COPY BY
JOHN VANDERBANK,
C.1694–1739,
AFTER UNKNOWN ARTIST.
(OPPOSITE)
HENRY V.
UNKNOWN ARTIST.

revolved around the theatre, Shakespeare moved his residence across the river. By 1599 he was living in Southwark, in the Liberty of the Clink, answerable to the Surrey authorities for the property taxes he was always slow to pay. It has become the tradition to see the actor-manager-writer, by now earning some £200 a year from the theatre, as tight-fisted. But 'habits of business,' as a Victorian biographer observed, 'are not incompatible with the possession of the highest genius.' Like most writers through the ages, Shakespeare was more likely impatient and inefficient about paperwork than a wilful tax-dodger. Writing two masterpieces a year, combing sources for inspiration while acting in the afternoons, does tend to clutter a desk.

The play most likely to have opened the Globe in the summer of 1599 is *Henry V*, whose opening Chorus contains an inaugural-sounding reference to 'this wooden O', within whose walls spectators are asked to lend their imaginations to 'piece out our imperfections with your thoughts'. Shakespeare had finished the play in a hurry amid rumours that the Master of the Revels would soon be prohibiting all re-enactment of English history on the stage. The Church was up in arms. A Cambridge lawyer named Hayward had published an ill-timed work on Henry Bolingbroke's deposition of Richard II, brazenly dedicated to the Earl of Essex. The Archbishop of Canterbury saw to it that the dedication was removed and the book – all 1,500 copies of it, along with others including, as it happened, the dread *Willobie his Avisa* – publicly burnt. Still on uncertain terms with his monarch, Essex was despatched at the end of March to quell the rebellious Irish.

But he would return in disgrace that September, just a week after Thomas Platter's visit to *Julius Caesar*. So, for once, we can be very precise about dates, only to boggle again at Shakespeare's fecundity. He must have completed *Henry V* between March 1599 and the Globe's opening that summer, when all English hearts would have been rooting for the huge forces rallied against the Irish. And he must obviously have written *Julius Caesar*, turning to the safer historical themes of ancient Rome, by the time of Platter's visit to the Globe that September. In between, his appetite for comedy perhaps whetted by the Queen's whim to see Falstaff in love, he completed two entertainments to

(OPPOSITE)
EDMUND KEAN AS
BRUTUS, FROM 'JULIUS
CAESAR'.
PAINTING BY
JAMES NORTHCOTE,
1746–1831.

which he gave the throwaway titles of *Much Ado About Nothing* and *As You Like It.*

For the setting of *Much Ado* he turned again to the landscape where he seems, in the right mood, to have felt so at home: Italy, specifically Sicily. Not that it matters. The intrigues between followers of Don Pedro, Prince of Aragon, his bastard half-brother Don John, and Leonato, Governor of Messina, might as well have happened anywhere. But the groundlings liked hot Mediterranean blood in their tales of passion, whether comic or tragic. The need for broad comedy to keep them happy also saw him introduce a memorably English character into the Italian landscape: Constable Dogberry, a parody of all those country law officers whose number had once included his father.

Shakespeare also wrote Dogberry as the requisite part for Will Kemp, resident company comedian since the death of Dick Tarleton ten years earlier. Now Kemp, too, quit the scene, if for rather different reasons. First, to make money, he would thrill the groundlings by morris-dancing, complete with cap and bells, all the way from London to Norwich; then the veteran comic would make his views public in *Kemp's Nine Daies Wonder*, a satire ridiculing the preening pretensions of writers like 'my notable Shakerags' and predicting their imminent demise. All this Italianate stuff, with its ornate classical references, wasn't a patch on the good old days of the Mystery plays, with their scope for the vaudeville-style slapstick at which he excelled, along with the delights of the ad-lib and laughing at your own jokes.

Shakespeare's relief is almost audible as Kemp's departure enables him to dispense with low comedy for its own sake. Now he could move on to deeper, darker comic creatures, the Fool in *King Lear* being an interim climax en route to Thersites, Autolycus and Caliban. With his next tragedy already germinating, he would signal as much with his homage to the memory of Tarleton as Yorick, and a pointed rebuke to the camp Kemp in Hamlet's instructions to the players.

In Kemp's replacement, Robert Armin, himself also a writer, Shakespeare was blessed with the perfect vehicle for the subtler strain of humour inaugurated by Touchstone and Feste, stepping-stones to Lear's fool. His relish in this new, more complex vein of humour is signalled in Jaques' description of

(PAGES 188–189)
LONDON FROM
SOUTHWARK, C.1650.
UNKNOWN ARTIST,
DUTCH SCHOOL.
(OPPOSITE)
KING LEAR.
PAINTING BY
PAUL FALCONER POOLE,
1807–79.

Touchstone as 'a material fool'. For Jaques' own immortal set-piece, another tribute to the theatre and its players, Shakespeare unabashedly used the Globe's own motto, *'Totus mundus agit histrionem'*, which translates almost literally as 'All the world's a stage . . . '

In the spirit of a production where backstage morale seems to have been running high, the playwright himself took on the tiny role of old Adam, the loyal retainer with the seasoned wisdom of every ancient servant throughout fiction. No doubt he took equal pleasure in honouring his mother – and recalling his happy childhood – by naming his own pastoral Utopia, where men 'fleet the time carelessly, as they did in the golden world', the Forest of Arden.

The civic unease bubbling beneath *Julius Caesar* reflected, by contrast, the nervous London summer of 1599, when talk of imminent Spanish invasion saw the gates of the capital locked and chains drawn across the streets against all comers. In this context, when unruly weather and hints of the supernatural portend disruption of the natural order, the Soothsayer takes on the broody millennial significance of a neo-Nostradamus.

In the central character of Brutus, 'the noblest Roman of them all', it is tempting to see Shakespeare still speaking up for the embattled Essex, whose undisguised ambition was now beginning to prove his downfall. Far from trouncing the Irish leader, Tyrone, he had concluded a truce with him; Essex returned from Ireland with a name for creating more knights among his followers than corpses amid the enemy. There were rumours that he had advised Tyrone of an imminent shift of power in England – of mutual advantage, perhaps, to them both. Intent on succeeding Elizabeth, the earl rashly confronted the Queen in her bedchamber, still mud-stained from his journey. No man had ever before been permitted to see the Virgin Queen in her nightgown, with her hair down, *sans* make-up. Within a matter of hours, unsurprisingly, Essex had been placed under arrest. The real surprise was that his charmed if wayward life had lasted so long.

That autumn saw Essex embark upon his last, suicidal adventure. Hauled before the Court of the Star Chamber on 29 November, he was kept under house arrest pending trial for 'maladministration' in Ireland. By

(OPPOSITE)
DOGBERRY EXAMINING CONRAD AND BORACHIO, FROM 'MUCH ADO ABOUT NOTHING', 1852. PAINTING BY HENRY STACEY MARKS, 1829–98.

February, to the anxiety of other courtiers, the Queen had taken pity upon her former favourite, and agreed to a Privy Council trial behind closed doors rather than a public examination in the Star Chamber. The following August she had Essex freed. In Ireland Lord Mountjoy was succeeding where he had failed, a public humiliation which the Queen seemed to consider punishment enough. But she hurt Essex's pride by banning him from court, and his wallet by depriving him of his monopoly of the import of sweet wines. In passionate letters, steeped in contrition, the desperate earl pleaded his case on both fronts. Her nerve steeled by the watchful Cecil, Raleigh and Francis Bacon, Elizabeth turned a deaf ear, threatening Essex with financial ruin by reverting his wine monopoly to the crown. Essex House now became a focus of dissent, as every discarded courtier and passed-over military man (precursors of Iago) rallied to his cause, urging him to take action before he was ruined.

On 6 February 1601 a group of Essex partisans, led by Sir Gelly Meyrick, came to the Globe with a request that the Lord Chamberlain's Men mount a performance of *Richard II* – complete with deposition scene – the following afternoon. In vain did the company protest that the play was past its prime, that it would scarcely fill the theatre. Did they realise the political significance, and thus the potential dangers, of what they were being asked to do? If so, as seems likely, they were careful to hide behind purely theatrical excuses. This particular play was 'so old and out of use', in Augustine Phillips' sworn testimony, as later reported by Bacon, 'that they should have small or no company at it.' But the conspirators offered to underwrite the performance, to the tune of 40 shillings beyond their 'ordinary' fee and box-office takings. Who were mere players to refuse such a lucrative commission from insistent eminences of high birth?

The following day, a Saturday, *Richard II* was duly played before a mix of restive groundlings and disenchanted aristocrats. Word of the special performance had spread round the city, where people were not slow to grasp its significance. Though not himself present, Essex was wilfully reminding the citizenry of a vivid precedent for the overthrow, and indeed assassination, of a capriciously favourite-prone monarch by a rejected nobleman – a terrible deed,

SIR WALTER RALEIGH,
C.1585.
PAINTING BY
NICHOLAS HILLIARD,
1547–1619.

to be sure, but a desperate act of *realpolitik* which had eventually bred a golden age.

The significance of that Saturday matinée did not escape Elizabeth, whose spies were everywhere. 'I am Richard II, know ye not that?' she declared. That same evening Essex was summoned to appear before the Privy Council; but he declined to leave the safety of his house, pleading that there was a plot to kill him, while in truth laying plans to seize the capital. The next morning, Sunday, saw a high-powered delegation including the Chief Justice, the Lord Keeper, the Earl of Worcester and Sir William Knollys descend on Essex House in the name of the Queen, to issue a stern warning against any potential act of treason. Confronted by an angry crowd, baying for their blood, the four notables found themselves taken hostage while Essex led two hundred troops in a mounted assault on the city.

But he found Ludgate locked against him, and the capital in no mood to rally to his cause. As a herald proclaimed him a traitor, some of his supporters fled; reinforcements promised from within the city did not materialise. Realising his cause was lost, Essex found his escape-route blocked by armed forces. There was a scuffle in which one of the Queen's men was killed, and one of his own taken prisoner, while Essex fought his way home via the river – only to find his hostages freed and his headquarters besieged. That evening, as the Lord Admiral threatened to blow up Essex House, the would-be usurper decided he had no option but to give himself up.

Receiving the news while dining alone, the Queen appeared unmoved. Next day she said simply: 'A senseless ingrate has at last revealed what has long been in his mind.' Brought to trial within a week, an insouciant Essex wore black – like the Danish prince then in the making – and quoted Shakespeare. 'I am indifferent how I speed,' he told the court. 'I owe God a death.' Says Prince Hal to Falstaff in *I Henry IV*, 'Why, thou owest God a death', to which Falstaff, left alone on the battlefield, replies with his great 'catechism': ''Tis not due yet ... '

But Essex's day, unlike Falstaff's, had come, and he faced it with cool, fatalistic indifference. On the day of his execution, 25 February (Ash Wednesday), he confided to Cecil: 'I must confess to you that I am the great-

(PAGES 196–197)
PRINCE HENRY AND
FALSTAFF, 1873.
PAINTING BY
LASLETT JOHN POTT,
1837–98.
(OPPOSITE)
ROBERT DEVEREUX,
2ND EARL OF ESSEX, 1597.
PAINTING BY
MARCUS GHEERAERTS
THE YOUNGER,
FL.1561; D.1635.

est, the most vilest, and the most unthankful traitor that ever has been in the land.' Granted his last wish – a private execution within the Tower, lest the acclaim of a baying mob corrupt him at the last – the thirty-four-year-old earl reportedly thanked God that he was 'thus spewed out of the realm'. The manner of Essex's death lingered in Shakespeare's mind five years later, when he had Malcolm report to his royal father of the execution of the Thane of Cawdor: 'Nothing in his life / Became him like the leaving it.'

The life of Shakespeare's friend Southampton, tried and condemned with Essex, was saved only by the intervention of his powerful and persuasive mother, the Dowager Countess. Moved by her pleas that her son was a biddable innocent, whose only fault was to have fallen into bad company, Cecil used his influence to have the earl's sentence commuted to indefinite imprisonment. Southampton was left languishing in the Tower. If there was something of Essex in Hamlet, there was something of Southampton in his loyal friend Horatio. But there was also something of Essex in Laertes, the courtier-turned-renegade who mounts his own reckless challenge against the throne.

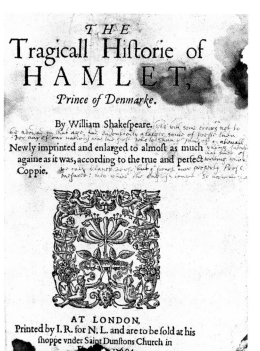

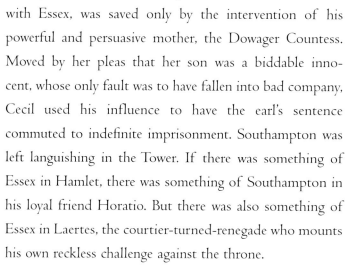
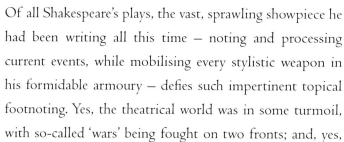
TITLE PAGE OF THE SECOND QUARTO
OF 'HAMLET', 1604.

Of all Shakespeare's plays, the vast, sprawling showpiece he had been writing all this time – noting and processing current events, while mobilising every stylistic weapon in his formidable armoury – defies such impertinent topical footnoting. Yes, the theatrical world was in some turmoil, with so-called 'wars' being fought on two fronts; and, yes, Shakespeare makes reference to them in Hamlet's discursive meditations on actors and acting. But only for dating purposes need we note Hamlet's grilling of Rosencrantz about the 'little eyases', the 'eyrie' of child-actors who irritated the established troupes by mounting a successful season of revenge tragedies at the Blackfriars in 1600–1. Amid 'much throwing about of brains', Hamlet is told, the effects had been felt even by 'Hercules and his load' – the Globe itself, that is, whose logo depicted Hercules bearing the world on his shoulders (as, in his way, does Hamlet). There is even a reference to the Lord Chamberlain's Men's brush with authority over that risky matinée of *Richard II*; when Hamlet asks why the approaching players are on the road – 'How chances it they travel?' – he is told that 'their inhibition comes by the means of the late innovation', i.e. Essex's uprising that February.

Already a stylistic war raged among the playwrights, a 'War of the Theatres', or *poetomachia*, in which Jonson, John Marston and Thomas Dekker vied to outdo each other with florid displays of dramatised learning in a series of *ad hominem* satires from 1599 to 1602, performed by the boys' companies. Now the actors were back on hard times, Hamlet is told, not 'followed' as once they were, because of a bunch of schoolchildren – through whom an opportunistic Jonson meanwhile waged war on Shakespeare by giving them plays such as *Cynthia's Revels*.

With his plays performed at court in preference to Jonson's, Shakespeare could afford to rise above the *poetomachia*, while deciding to turn necessity to definitive advantage. Revenge tragedies were suddenly all the rage, and not just in the box-office predominance of the Paul's Boys at the Blackfriars. The tradition begun by Aeschylus and Seneca was undergoing a revival sparked by Kyd's *Spanish Tragedy* and Shakespeare's own *Titus Andronicus*. Now Marston was enjoying a huge success with *Antonio's Revenge*, soon to be followed by Tourneur's *The Revenger's Tragedy* and Webster's *The Duchess of Malfi*. So Shakespeare would write the most ambitious revenge tragedy of them all, turning to his advantage the perennial problem of plot construction: given the catalytic murder revealed in the first act, and the requisite revenge-killing in the last, what do you do in the intervening three? Take the form head-on, he decided, and create a philosopher-revenger who spends those three acts and more crippled by moral doubts and mortal fears.

Coming at roughly the half-way point of his output, *Hamlet* marks a sea-change in Shakespeare's view of himself and his abilities. Everything he had written suddenly seems like preparation for this moment, as he reaches higher and wider than ever before, going out of his way to show off every aspect of his consummate art, dazzling his audience with flights of fancy and psycho-analytical wisdom whose mysteries will never be fully fathomed. This dizzying

display of poetry and philosophy, wit and insight, finds its central focus in one man, one very mortal man, perhaps the most complex creation in literary history, in whom every subsequent generation has found multiple reflections of itself.

Not merely is *Hamlet* Shakespeare's longest play, and technically his most ambitious. As it lurches from comedy to tragedy, high art to low, violence to stillness, love to hatred, confusion to redemption, it tells the story of Everyman as never before or since, distilling as much individual and collective experience as can be contained in one frail, confused man of action, a poet-philosopher confronting all our own everyday problems while trying to solve one none of us will ever have to face.

Hamlet is the launch-pad for a quite different, more profound and multi-layered Shakespeare from the merely talented and versatile dramatist we have known so far. Henceforth he will demonstrate the eternal frailties of humankind, by telling the stories of mighty men in terms of their mortal failings. It is as if the Stratford man suddenly lost patience with the petty squabbling around him — the snobbish disputes between university-educated playwrights and their peers, the eternal woes of the actor-managers and impresarios, the shifting tensions between the Queen and her courtiers — and lifted the art of drama onto an entirely new and far higher plane. *Hamlet* is the unilateral declaration of independence which marks the birth of the Jacobean Shakespeare, the author of *Othello* and *Macbeth*, *Lear* and those last plays in which tragic events breed built-in redemption.

In barely ten years he had already raised English drama from crude comedy, lumbering history and murderous melodrama to a level of intelligence, honesty, wit and humanity unmatched in any other era, before or since. Four hundred years later, at the end of the twentieth century, *Hamlet* speaks as vividly as it ever has to each succeeding generation, all of whom see almost too much of themselves in its 'mirror, held, as 'twere, up to nature'. Denmark was also a country suddenly — and unusually — on people's lips. Since the death of Essex, the perennial question of the Virgin Queen's heir had focused more than ever around the Scottish king, James, whose wife was a Danish princess, and a Catholic, named Anne. Beyond such localised perspectives, Shakespeare seems

(OPPOSITE)
THE ACTOR JOSEPH
TALMA, 1763–1826,
IN THE ROLE OF HAMLET.
PAINTING BY
ANTHELME FRANCOIS
LAGRENEE, 1774–1832.

to have been in nostalgic mood while writing what he must have known was his masterpiece.

The memory of his own son Hamnet lends the play's parallel father-son relationships an especially poignant charge; in the Warwickshire dialect of the day, Hamnet and Hamlet were, in effect, the same name. In the Ghost of Hamlet's Father – the part he himself played – Shakespeare meanwhile seems to be paying tribute to his own, now a shadow of his former self, on the very threshold of that bourn from which no traveller returns.

On 8 September 1601 Shakespeare was back in Stratford, to bury his father in the churchyard of Holy Trinity. John Shakespeare had lived into his seventies, a mighty age for the time, but we know little of his fortunes beyond his middle years. Most of his friends had long since quit the scene, by now as fond a memory as his own prominence as a civic leader; but we can be sure that in later life the retired glover enjoyed a certain dignity around town as a local eminence, relishing the reflected glory of a son making a name for himself in the capital, new owner of the biggest house in town.

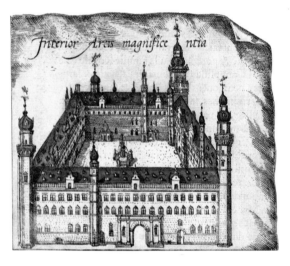

VIEW OF KRONBORG CASTLE, ELSINORE,
SETTING FOR 'HAMLET' C.1590.
ENGRAVING BY GEORG BRAUN.

Now head of the family, William seems to have been no different from most sons in regarding his father's death as a singular reminder of his own mortality. It was perhaps at this moment, plunged into a predictable bout of melancholy, that he felt confirmed in discarding any vestigial religious belief. The fatalism of *Hamlet*, so appealing to the existential angst of four centuries of adolescents, now curdles to the bleak nihilism of *Troilus and Cressida*, the darkest, most pessimistic play he ever wrote. Shakespeare took the ancient legend of the war-separated lovers, which he had known in Chaucer's version since his schooldays, and turned it into more than a mere indictment of inconstancy, or just another fable of man's inhumanity to man. In this work more than any other, a broad array of characters – most of them worldly leaders – fail to live up to their own ideals. They are all talk and no action, until eventually goaded by the basest of motives, a far remove

(OPPOSITE)
PORTRAIT OF HENRY V,
1387–1422.
PAINTING BY
BENJAMIN BURNELL,
1769–1828.

from the ideals they claim to represent. Few have many redeeming features. The only character in the entire play who remains true to himself throughout, and consistently speaks the most sense, is the cynical, vagabond clown Thersites — another great part for Robert Armin.

Of all Shakespeare's plays, *Troilus and Cressida* has been uniquely adopted by the twentieth century, apparently the first since Shakespeare's day to find sombre echoes of itself in his cerebral vision of a world collapsed by war. It has enjoyed a rebirth since the Second World War, as central a member of the core repertoire as any of its better-known siblings. At the time, the indications are that *Troilus and Cressida* did less well at the Globe than in private performances for well-educated lawyers and courtiers. In this vein, while *Hamlet* continued to pack them in, Shakespeare kept his Chaucer at his elbow (and his Bible still in mind) for a personal homage to *The Parlement of Fowles* in his next published work, untitled but traditionally known as 'The Phoenix and Turtle'. A sixty-seven-line elegy in trochaic tetrameter, it was appended with other 'commendatory' poems by Jonson, Marston and Chapman to *Love's Martyr*, or *Rosalin's Complaint* by Robert Chester, subtitled as 'allegorically shadowing the truth of love, in the constant fate of the phoenix and turtle'.

After the Herculean effort of *Hamlet*, his productivity rate slowed appreciably. Another *annus mirabilis* lay just ahead, but the first years of the new century see his output halve, albeit briefly, to just one play a year. Uniquely, in this mid-period of his career, he also deigned to stoop to collaboration. He had shared writing credits with others at the start of his career, and would

THE BEAR GARDEN AND
GLOBE THEATRE ON
BANKSIDE.
UNATTRIBUTED
ENGRAVING FROM
VENETIAN MAP, 1816.

relax into partnership again at the end; at the height of his powers, for the most part, he left teamwork to others, notably Dekker, Middleton and Webster, even Jonson (who joined hands with Chapman and Marston on *Eastward Ho!*). But now, as Elizabeth's glorious reign drew inexorably towards its close, Shakespeare was persuaded to undertake some rescue work on a piece which, because of its delicate subject-matter, had fallen foul of the censor.

Sir Edmund Tilney, Master of the Revels, had demanded extensive cuts and alterations to Anthony Munday's play about Sir Thomas More. In the case of the man who had so famously crossed the Queen's beloved father, royal sensitivities were very much at stake. Dekker became involved, as did Heywood, picking their way tactfully around the question of the (unspecified) 'articles' to which More declined to subscribe; no fewer than five different hands have made additions to the original manuscript, still to be seen in the British Library, complete with Tilney's complaints. Among them, by general consent, is that of Shakespeare. Hand D, in folios 8 and 9, is the only example of his handwriting we possess, beyond the five or six authentic signatures.

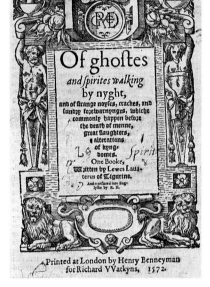

TITLE PAGE OF 'OF GHOSTES AND
SPIRITES WALKING BY NIGHT',
TRANSLATED BY
ROBERT HARRISON, 1572.

With their paymasters away on tour, and the Admiral's men waiting for Henslowe to complete work on his new playhouse, it was only natural that his rival playwrights should turn in desperation to the colleague who was also a stakeholder in the Lord Chamberlain's Men. He was now an independent writer of means with no need to collaborate for mere pecuniary gain. But the conscience of the Catholic martyr was a subject with an obvious appeal to Shakespeare, even if his own faith had lapsed. The consciences of noble minds prepared to pay the supreme price was a theme which had preoccupied him since *Julius Caesar*, and would sustain him through *Macbeth* and beyond.

On 2 February 1602, Candlemas Day, the law student John Manningham attended a feast at the Middle Temple, followed by an entertainment from the Lord Chamberlain's Men. 'We had a play called Twelfth Night or what you will,' Manningham recorded in his diary. On 6 January the previous year,

Twelfth Night 1601, Elizabeth I had commanded the Lord Chamberlain's Men to stage a play at her Whitehall palace to mark the state visit of Don Virginio Orsino, Duke of Bracciano, a small province of western Italy. Did Shakespeare take the name of the Queen's VIP guest in vain, by making him the lovesick Duke of Illyria? Did he call the play *Twelfth Night* (or, *What You Will*) because no other title suggested itself? All three of his mid-period comedies have throwaway titles. The name of the piece performed that night was not entered in the court record; but the Duke wrote home to his wife that he was feted with 'a mixed comedy with pieces of music and dances'.

Though a popular hit in Shakespeare's lifetime, *Twelfth Night* somehow seems to have escaped publication, first appearing in print in the First Folio of 1623. As it took its place in the Globe's popular repertoire, Shakespeare's stake-holding was beginning to pay dividends. On 1 May 1602 he paid the considerable sum of £320 – almost as much as he had paid for New Place – to William Combe and his nephew John for one hundred and seven acres of arable land in 'old' Stratford, farming country to the north of the town. He did not trouble to return home for the transaction, delegating his brother Gilbert to represent him at the formal handover of the four 'yardlands'. Six months later, that October, he also purchased a cottage on the south side of Chapel Lane, across the road from New Place, apparently as the home for a gardener.

At the end of 1602, a humdrum writing year by his standards, it is intriguing that Shakespeare's mind was as much on his Stratford landholdings as on his work. As both poet and dramatist, he seems to have become becalmed. It is almost as if he required some new impetus, perhaps from the exterior world beyond his own, to renew his creative energies and drive him forward to a new phase of work, a new level of achievement. Very much a creature of his times, as well as eternally above them, he found just such a stimulus in the momentous events of early 1603 – long awaited, but no less for that an upheaval of state.

On 2 February 1603 the Lord Chamberlain's Men performed before their Queen for what proved to be the last time. Six weeks later, on 24 March, after a forty-five-year reign which still ranks among the most glorious in English history, Elizabeth I finally breathed her last.

(OPPOSITE)
QUEEN ELIZABETH I
IN CORONATION ROBES,
C.1559.
ENGLISH SCHOOL,
SIXTEENTH CENTURY.
PAGES 210–211
THE 'WOODEN O'.
THE GLOBE THEATRE,
SOUTHWARK.

VIII

THE KING'S MAN

1603–1606

Shakespeare's great burst of
self-confidence may have driven him
perilously close to the royal bone,
suggesting that kings need to be told harsh
truths by their licensed retainers,
and stripped of their creature comforts
to appreciate that they are, in the end,
as much of a 'poor, bare, fork'd animal'
as their humblest subject.

*E*xeunt the Tudors; enter the Stuarts. Not until she was on her deathbed did Elizabeth finally deign to name her heir, whispering to attendant Privy Councillors that she could not be possibly be succeeded by anyone but a king – 'and who should that be but our cousin of Scotland?' Horsemen rushed the news to Edinburgh, whence King James VI of Scotland and now I of England embarked on a triumphal progress south.

Two years younger than Shakespeare, James was a cultivated but graceless, self-indulgent man, fond of his pleasures, not least food and wine – which he preferred served to him on bended knee, preferably by the barons who vied to entertain him in splendour on his stately six-week journey to London. En route the new king dispensed justice as liberally as honours, creating no fewer than three hundred new knights while straining to appear even-handed with offenders against the law. In Newark, on 21 April, he magnanimously freed all the prisoners in the castle while ordering the immediate execution, without trial, of a cutpurse caught red-handed in the crowd struggling for a glimpse of him. Such extremes of justice and mercy gave Shakespeare ideas, as did James's reluctance to put his royal personage on show to the common people. Already the King was offering the playwright material for the new work his company would perform before him the following Christmas.

Within ten days of arriving in London, although besieged by other claims for his attention, the new king took the Lord Chamberlain's troupe under his own royal patronage. Shakespeare was now one of the King's Men. He is named in the royal warrant prepared on James's instructions by Keeper of the Privy Seal, Lord Cecil, and issued under the Great Seal of England on 17 May 1603.

By taking them under his royal wing, James had officially confirmed the standing of the Lord Chamberlain's Men as the leading theatrical company in the land. And James was to prove a valuable patron to Shakespeare and his fellows. In the thirteen years between his accession and the poet's death, the King's Men would play at court no fewer than 187 times – an average of thirteen royal command performances a year, compared with three during Elizabeth's reign. He paid twice as much, what's more, reckoning his post-prandial entertainment a legitimate drain on the Privy Purse. For the King's

(PAGE 212)
KING JAMES I OF
ENGLAND AND VI OF
SCOTLAND, 1621.
PAINTING BY DANIEL
MYTENS, C.1590–1648.
(OPPOSITE)
OTHELLO, DESDEMONA
AND IAGO.
PAINTING BY HENRY
MUNRO, 1791–1814.

Men, this meant gainful employment even when the theatres were closed by the plague – as, for instance, that August, when they were paid £21 12s to entertain the new Spanish ambassador, Don Juan Fernandez de Velasco, at Somerset House. As the upper crust then evacuated London for the duration, which turned out to be almost a year, the king repaired to Wilton House, near Salisbury, as a guest of the Countess of Pembroke. In the autumn of 1603 his players were summoned to perform *As You Like It* there, for which they were paid the munificent sum of £30. 'We have the man Shakespeare with us,' the Countess wrote to her son William, eponymous patron of the Earl of Pembroke's Men.

Pembroke's mother, the Dowager Countess, was the sister of the late Sir Philip Sidney, herself cultivated enough to have edited his Sonnet sequence *Astrophel and Stella* after his death at the Battle of Zutphen. Now forty-two, still renowned as a beauty to be reckoned with, she loved the theatre enough to have tried her own hand as a playwright. During this sojourn, therefore, she might well have shown the man Shakespeare her own modest effort, *Antonius*, adapted from the *Marc-Antoine* of the French Senecan Robert Garnier.

Whether or not she gave Shakespeare the idea for a play about Antony and Cleopatra, the formidable Countess certainly inspired a distinctive figure at the heart of his work-in-progress. Or so George Bernard Shaw believed, whatever admirers of Juliet or Portia, Rosalind or Cleopatra may think of Shaw's claim that the Countess of Rousillon in *All's Well That Ends Well* is 'the most charming of all his women, young or old'. Her son Bertram spurns an arranged marriage, just like the Countess of Pembroke's own son, not to mention that other nobleman who weaves in and out of Shakespeare's life, the Earl of Southampton. For another comedy with another throwaway name, so elegant as to have been written more for private than public performance, he was again treating of matters uncomfortably close to home.

The deserted wife who overcomes impossible odds to regain her husband is as ancient a motif, dating back to the Greek myths, as the corrupt ruler who perverts justice to gratify his lust. In *Measure for Measure*, Shakespeare's mood grows even darker, weaving religious language and imagery into a work

(PAGES 216–217)
OTHELLO.
PAINTING BY
SEBASTIANO NOVELLI,
1853–1916.
(OPPOSITE)
'I AM NEVER MERRY WHEN
I HEAR SWEET MUSICK',
FROM 'THE MERCHANT OF
VENICE', 1888.
PAINTING BY
SIR JOHN EVERETT
MILLAIS,
1829–96.

obsessed with sex, hypocrisy and death. As it moves between Angelo's inner sanctum, a prison and a brothel, this remains one of the most cerebral of all Shakespeare's works, while also one of the most sexually charged. Chaste and virtuous to the point of priggishness, Isabella is about to enter a convent when her brother Claudio is cruelly condemned to death for impregnating his bride-to-be; Angelo's insistence on her sexual favours in return for her brother's life is played out on a plane high above Shakespeare's immediate source: the tale of Juriste, Epitia and her brother Vico in a dramatisation of his own novella by the Italian poet Giovanni Batista Cinthio, who would also provide the inspiration for Shakespeare's next, equally sex-obsessed work.

In the year from November 1604 to 31 October 1605, according to the accounts of the Master of the Revels, Shakespeare and the King's Men performed at court at least eleven times – ten different plays, including seven by Shakespeare, mostly hardy annuals from *The Comedy of Errors* and *Love's Labour's Lost* to *The Merry Wives of Windsor*. The one play James specifically asked to see twice was *The Merchant of Venice*. In *Measure for Measure*, Shakespeare was again taking risks: gratifying the King's interest in justice and mercy while chronicling his own disenchantment with both.

As a comedy, his twelfth, it seems to end a line of dramatic inquiry he had been pursuing throughout the fifteen or so years of his writing career, refining it to the point where the twentieth century has trouble calling this a comedy, preferring to label it a 'problem' play. Its bleak mood and savage humour – a comedy which takes place almost entirely in darkness, shadows or dingy interiors – suggests Shakespeare felt he had mined this vein to its very core, to what he considered a natural conclusion. The problems posed by the final scene further suggest that, immersed in Cinthio, he was already brooding about *Othello*.

Measure for Measure was the last comedy Shakespeare would write. The great tragedies immediately ahead were already taking shape in his mind.

'Let's kill all the lawyers,' he had written as early as 2 *Henry VI*. As he worked on this last statement on the law and its administrators, steeped in disillusion with both, Shakespeare was venting a personal as well as philosophical rage.

The law's failure to protect a writer's copyright continued to plague him, as the appearance of a 'bad' quarto of *Hamlet* in 1603 now moved his company — not the playwright himself — to supervise the publication of a revised, more accurate text, thus sparing posterity the laughable 1603 'memorial reconstruction' of the most famous speech in all literature.

Legal niceties meanwhile continued to dog his business dealings back in Stratford. That spring he felt obliged to sue his neighbour Philip Rogers, an apothecary, for payment of a paltry debt barely exceeding £2; having sold Rogers twenty bushels of malt, and then lent him two shillings, Shakespeare had received only six shillings in repayment. He demanded ten shillings damages on top of the 35s 10d due. There is no record how the court ruled, or that he ever received his due; but this would not be the last time he chose to pursue debtors. At the same time, ironically, he was living in London amid domestic complexities which would return to torment him in the shape of a protracted lawsuit — not, for once, as plaintiff or defendant, this time as a character witness.

During the plague year of 1604 Shakespeare was lodging in Silver Street, Cripplegate, with a family named Mountjoy. He had probably known them some years, as he had given their Huguenot name to the French herald in *Henry V*, written as he and the Globe had crossed the river in 1599. Probably he met them through his friend Richard Field, the printer from Stratford, who lived over his own shop in nearby Wood Street, and whose French wife Jacqueline would have worshipped alongside Mary Mountjoy at London's French church. Why and when Shakespeare moved back across the river, to this north-west corner of the city walls, we do not know; the plague may well have been cause enough, and it would seem no coincidence that his colleagues and friends John Heminges and Henry Condell lived nearby, in the next-door parish of St Mary's, Aldermanbury.

Silver Street was the centre of the lucrative wig industry, once patronised by the late Queen herself; from Ben Jonson we know the delicious details that 'her teeth were made in Blackfriars, both her eyebrows in the Strand, and her

Ham. **To** be, or not to be, I there's the point,
To Die, to sleepe, is that all? I all:
No, to sleepe, to dreame, I mary there it goes,
For in that dreame of death, when wee awake,
And borne before an euerlasting Iudge,
From whence no passenger euer retur'nd,
The vndiscouered country, at whose sight
The happy smile, and the accursed damn'd.
But for this, the ioyfull hope of this,
Whol'd beare the scornes and flattery of the world,
Scorned by the right rich, the rich curssed of the poore?

'TO BE OR NOT TO BE' AS REMEMBERED BY
UNSCRUPULOUS ACTORS ASSISTING THE 'PIRATE'
PUBLISHER OF THE 1603 'BAD' QUARTO OF HAMLET

(OPPOSITE)
PORTIA, FROM 'THE
MERCHANT OF VENICE'.
PAINTING BY
CHARLES EDWARD
PERUGINI,
1839–1918.

hair in Silver Street.' Shakespeare's landlord, Christopher Mountjoy, was a prosperous maker of 'tires', or expensively jewelled adornments for the head-gear of well-to-do ladies. In 1604, while Shakespeare lived under their roof, the Mountjoys' daughter – Mary, like her mother – was being courted by one of her father's apprentices, Stephen Belott. The Mountjoys approved of the match, but Belott was holding out for a larger dowry, so Shakespeare was asked to intervene. The poet succeeded in negotiating a financial settlement to the satisfaction of both parties – £60 on the celebration of the nuptials and £200 on Mountjoy's death, according to Belott – and the couple were married on 19 November at the parish church of St Olave.

That might have been the end of the matter – and no more than a tanta-

SILVER STREET,
CRIPPLEGATE. FROM A
MAP ATTRIBUTED TO
RALPH AGAS, 1633.

(OPPOSITE)
SCENE FROM
'CORIOLANUS', 1797.
PAINTING BY
SIR FRANCIS BOURGEOIS,
1756–1811.

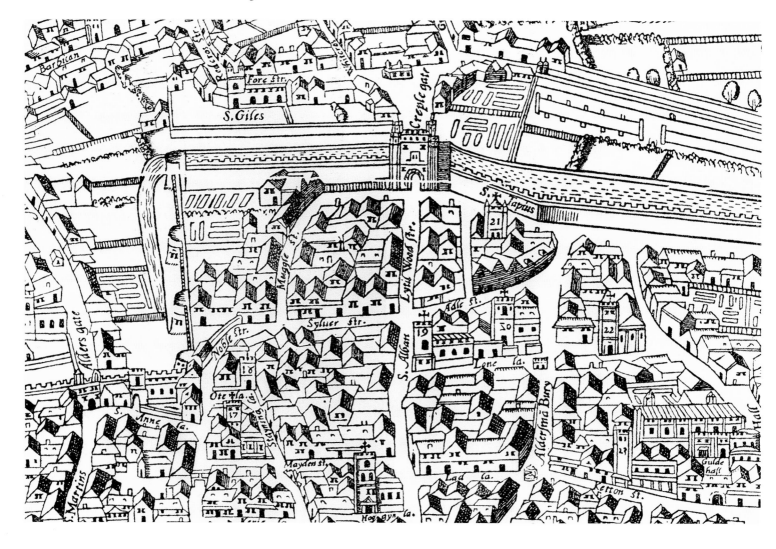

lising glimpse of Shakespeare playing reluctant Pandarus — had not both parties reneged on the deal. Instead of staying on in Silver Street as expected, presumably to inherit the family business, Belott took Mary off to start up a rival emporium, hiring an apprentice of his own; so the enraged Mountjoy handed over a mere £10, throwing in some sticks of old furniture and a random assortment of cast-off chattels from worn blankets to a small pair of scissors. In vain did Mountjoy's wife plead with him to treat their daughter better; but the elder Mary's death less than two years later, in 1606, effected a temporary *rapprochement*. The Belotts moved back in to look after her widowed father, and did indeed become his partners in the business. All too soon they fell out again; Belott flounced out, taking his wife with him; the elderly Mountjoy was left alone to drown his sorrows. By 1612, when Shakespeare was back in Stratford, rumours reached Belott that the embittered, ever more dissolute old man, who was anyway drinking away his inheritance, intended to cut him off without a penny.

So poor Shakespeare was summoned to London to give evidence in a court case attempting to establish the truth of the original marital settlement. By now it was all of eight years ago, and his memory was hazy. While describing the apprentice Belott, in his deposition, as 'a very good and industrious servant' who 'did well and honestly behave himself', the poet recalled the sum due as £50, and had no recollection of the £200 supposedly promised on Mountjoy's death. In the matter of Belott v Mountjoy the Court of Requests adjourned for a month, asking Shakespeare to reappear for further examination; but the second time around he did not show up. It was all so long ago, and he'd had a lifetime of lawyers. The court eventually took a dim view of the conduct of both the irascible father and the erratic son-in-law, and split the difference by awarding Belott twenty nobles, or £6 13s 4d. There is no record that Mountjoy ever paid up.

This tawdry domestic drama, the stuff of a kith-and-kin farce if he had not long ago left such antics behind him, offers a touching vignette of Shakespeare as the amenable lodger — 'a man among men', as he has been described in this context — willing to lend a hand in sorting out another family's problems. But this glimpse ahead to the elderly playwright, losing his

(PAGES 226–227)
OPHELIA, FROM
'HAMLET', 1914.
PAINTING BY
STEPHEN REID
1873–1948.
(OPPOSITE)
WILLIAM SHAKESPEARE,
C.1610.
PAINTING ATTRIBUTED TO
JOHN TAYLOR, D.1651.

memory, irritated to be summoned up and down to London from the peace of his rural retirement, assumes a particular poignancy in 1604, when this sorry saga started. For the year of his fortieth birthday was certainly a watershed in his life, when a sudden change of dramatic gear suggests a sense of physical as well as mental foreboding.

Still acting as well as writing — the records show him onstage in Jonson's *Sejanus* in 1603 — the poet-actor-playwright was certainly driving himself as hard as ever. He was as prone as any Londoner to the effects of too much liquor — water was not yet drinkable, tea had not become the English way — and too many carbohydrates. But there is no need to take too anxious a cholesterol count; Shakespeare sounds like less of a glutton than Jonson. Even Falstaff's over-eating was largely confined to high-protein capons, though Hal does tick him off over too much 'sugar-candy'; nourishing pippins and cheese are served in *The Merry Wives of Windsor*, root vegetables in Timon of Athens' cave; Macbeth seems to speak for a 'nothing to excess' regime on Shakespeare's part when he toasts his dinner guests: 'Now good digestion wait on appetite, / And health on both.'

If Shakespeare was developing problems, they were more spiritual than physical. As he turned forty, the world was too much with him. The exuberant gaiety of his early work is no more. His last plays to be called comedies are the work of a gravely reflective man, nostalgic for times past, not so much cynical as sceptical, more battle-hardened than world-weary, old before his time.

Forty was quite an age for the day, five years beyond the average life expectancy, especially for those choosing the lawless, polluted, disease-ridden life of the capital. Where his soul had been scarred by the death of his son, the demise of his father had merely aged him. The natural *joie de vivre* had gone, to return only fitfully in his writings, replaced by the more sombre, searching spirit of inquiry which would now produce his mature masterworks.

Whatever else was troubling him, Shakespeare next chose to address a subject unexplored in any of his previous twenty-six plays, but to which he would return, as if obsessively: sexual jealousy. Whether reading or watching

(OPPOSITE)
DESDEMONA KNEELING
AT HER FATHER'S FEET,
FROM 'OTHELLO', 1852.
PAINTING BY
EUGENE DELACROIX,
1798–1863.

Othello and *The Winter's Tale*, or indeed lingering over the Sonnets, it is hard to resist the conclusion that the poet capable of evoking the 'green-eyed monster' in such violent language must have experienced its unique horrors himself.

Nor can we think for a moment that it was caused by his long-distance wife Anne, with some observers (including James Joyce's Stephen Dedalus) who have gone so far as to suggest that Shakespeare's brother Richard had done the poet's office betwixt his sheets. The Dark Lady was as good for sexual jealousy as for the clap — more so, perhaps, than other London women of easy virtue. But who might have caused him such powerful emotions at this particular time, feeding the frenzy behind Othello's 'goats and monkeys'? Who, for one, but the indirect cause of his future legal woes, Mary Mountjoy senior?

Cuckoldry at court tends to survive the vagaries of time, living on in diaries and letters to shiver the reputations of those involved; further down the social scale, it takes some freak event for guilty secrets to survive four hundred years and more. Unfortunately for Mary Mountjoy, she chose to consult the physician-astrologer Simon Forman, an assiduous keeper of notebooks, on discovering that she was pregnant by a neighbour named Henry Wood, a mercer and trader in cloths around the corner in Swan Alley. 'Mary Mountjoy alained' (or 'concealed'), reads Forman's cryptic note — preserved in the Bodleian Library, Oxford, along with his jottings on Richard Burbage's wife Winifred, and indeed Philip Henslowe, whom he treated in 1597 for 'tingling and itching in his head' and 'much melancholy'.

Just as well, for Mary Mountjoy's pregnancy proved to be a false alarm. So her marriage survived to see the younger Mary marry the apprentice, with all that followed. Was Mary senior flighty enough to seduce her lodger — himself not averse, as we shall see, to taking advantage of his landladies — and then to torment him with her attentions to Wood or indeed her husband? Had she and Shakespeare secretly been lovers for five years or more before he moved in, the name of Mountjoy in *Henry V* being his coded thanks for her flirtatious help with the play's adventures in French? Or did Christopher Mountjoy pour out to his long-suffering lodger the agonies of knowing his wife was in love elsewhere?

These are passing thoughts, no more, for Shakespeare himself surely

(OPPOSITE)
SIR ROBERT CECIL,
1ST EARL OF SALISBURY,
1602.
PAINTING BY
JOHN DE CRITZ
THE ELDER,
C.1555–1641.

1600

ABDVLGVAHID.

ÆTATIS:42.

LEGATVS REGIS BARBAF
IN ANGLIAM.

THE MOORISH
AMBASSADOR TO QUEEN
ELIZABETH'S COURT,
1600—1, WHILE
SHAKESPEARE WAS
WRITING 'OTHELLO'.

knew enough of the pangs of jealousy before moving in with the Mountjoys. The later Sonnets are full of the agonies which would now shudder so terribly through *Othello*. He had also been a player at court four years earlier during a prolonged visit by the Moorish ambassador of the King of Barbary, an exotic figure who attracted much attention; he and his Muslim retinue, being 'strange in their ways', were naturally described as 'Barbarians'. A portrait of the ambassador painted during his visit, and inscribed '*Legatus regis barbariae in Angliam*', settles the age-old debate about the precise ethnic background Shakespeare intended to convey by the word Moor. 'Is it too fanciful,' asks one of the play's most recent editors, 'to suppose that this very face haunted Shakespeare's imagination and inspired the writing of his tragedy?'

'No nation in the world is so subject unto jealousy, for they will rather lose their lives than put up any disgrace in the behalf of their women' wrote John Leo, a Barbary-bred Moor, of his 'very proud and high-minded, and wonderfully addicted unto wrath' fellow-countrymen. 'Their wits are but mean, and they are so credulous that they will believe matters impossible which are told them.' Shakespeare plays with time, with class, nobility, credulity, domesticity, with the concepts of knowledge and honesty; but in *Othello* he creates the first example of a 'noble' black man, however fallible, in Western literature. At a time when Sir Robert Cecil was hearing protests about the number of blackamoors 'infiltrating' English society, it was (to say the least) bold of Shakespeare to make a noble non-savage the most sympathetic of all his tragic heroes – as enlightened on racial prejudice, as pioneeringly anti-bigotry, as he had been in *The Merchant of Venice*.

In Iago he fashions the most diabolical of all his images of evil incarnate, made all the more chilling for the fact that, unlike Richard III and Aaron, he does not kill anyone – except by proxy. The ensign's supposed motives for poisoning his master's mind against his bride – that he had been passed over for the lieutenantship, that Othello had seduced his own wife – are so inadequate (the latter stretching even his own belief) as to take on the eeriest notes of bewildered, almost apologetic self-justification. Coleridge's famous verdict, 'the motive-hunting of motiveless malignity', has never been bettered.

In the absence of any supernatural element (as in *Hamlet* and *Macbeth*), or extreme psychological disturbance (as in *Lear*), *Othello* remains the most intimate, the most direct of Shakespeare's four great tragedies. It is as a private, not as a public man that its protagonist is undone, causing passing political embarrassment to the state to which he has done some service, but no great disruption of the natural order. Lacking the metaphysical complexities of *Hamlet* or *Lear*, the play can often have a more direct impact on audiences. When one of the great nineteenth-century Othellos, William Macready, took

Iago by the throat, a gentleman in the audience could bear it all no longer, and famously cried out: 'Choke the devil! Choke him!'

Was the King offended by *Othello* when it was performed before him on 1 November 1604? We have no reason to suppose so. But the name of Iago, of course, means James — in Spanish, moreover, the language of England's old enemy, while the names of all the play's other Venetians are appropriately Italian.

If *Othello* took liberties with the King's name, *King Lear* mocked his love of flattery and the Scottish play to follow held uneasy, home-based echoes of a recent attempt on his life. No, James was too self-admiring to take offence at nuances in *Othello* and *Lear*, too cultured a theatre-lover to derive anything but sheer pleasure from his very own acting troupe's prolific and erudite playwright. Shakespeare's great burst of self-confidence may have driven him perilously close to the royal bone, suggesting that kings need to be told harsh truths by their licensed retainers, and stripped of their creature comforts to appreciate that they are, in the end, as much of a 'poor, bare, fork'd animal' as their humblest subject.

WILLIAM MACREADY AS OTHELLO.
ENGRAVING AFTER TRACEY.

But the play's most interesting exterior references are to himself. If he is playing the Fool to James's Lear, he is even more playing the real-life father tragically deprived of his beloved son, and pouring all his paternal love, sharpened by years of guilty absenteeism, into his daughters. Only twice more, in *Coriolanus* and *The Winter's Tale*, would Shakespeare give his protagonists an even remotely significant son, in each case still children, as if young Hamnets frozen in time. The emphasis from *Lear* onwards is otherwise exclusively, almost obsessively, on daughters. Her purity intensified by her evil sisters, Cordelia is the forerunner of Marina, Imogen, Perdita and Miranda. Shakespeare's mind was on his own daughters, Susanna and Judith, now twenty-two and twenty, and far the most eligible young women in Stratford.

With their dowries also in mind, perhaps, he now set about enlarging his Warwickshire property portfolio, this time with a huge purchase. On 24 July 1605 he spent no less than £440 on 'tithes of corn, grain, blade and hay' in the town itself, old Stratford, Welcombe and Bishopston. New Place had cost less than a seventh as much. Shakespeare had bided his time before acting on that advice seven years before from Abraham Sturley, on a hint from Adrian Quiney, that tithes might be a good investment. In the deeds of purchase from Ralph Hubaud of Ipsley, a former county sheriff, we catch tantalising glimpses of Shakespeare's true and trusty Stratford friends. Again a witness, as he had been three years earlier to the poet's last land purchase, was Anthony Nash of Welcombe, to whom Shakespeare would entrust the collection of his rents, and whose son would marry the poet's granddaughter; another was the lawyer handling the transaction, Francis Collins. Both would be remembered in Shakespeare's will, which Collins himself oversaw.

By 1605, four years after his father's death, Shakespeare had rebuilt his family's fortunes. The residence in Henley Street now known as The Birthplace; the handsome spread flourishing around New Place, complete with full-time gardener; extensive landholdings within the town and all around it: this was an estate more than substantial enough to ensure his family's future. At the age of forty-one, he need never work again. So this is the moment when we can reflect, with as much relief as satisfaction, that mean-minded tradition has got it wrong. Shakespeare did not write plays only for the money. There was plenty more he wanted to say.

Shakespeare was also at the height of his fame. London publishers felt free to attach his name to any old play in the hope of boosting sales. In 1595 and 1602 they had merely attached the initials W.S. to apocryphal works such as *Locrine* and *Thomas Lord Cromwell*; now, in 1605, the full name of William Shakespeare was brazenly appended to another play he did not write, *The London Prodigal*, as it would be again in 1608 to another called *A Yorkshire Tragedy*. Far from writing one of these routine, bums-on-seats comedies of manners or tear-jerking bodice-rippers, Shakespeare was at the time completing the most intricate, profound and perplexing work he would ever lay before an audience.

Since the previous year, 1604, King James's central political priority had been a sustained campaign to persuade the English parliament to endorse a formal union with Scotland. In speech after speech he made repeated reference to the troubles brought upon early Britain by its divisions. Shakespeare, insofar as he was a political animal, seems to have been pro-union; the central theme of James's speeches certainly chimed with the sustained motif in his own work of the disruption of the natural order brought about by division and disunion.

All Shakespeare's previous work came together in *King Lear* — his most intense and passionate meditation on love, mortality, kingship, ingratitude, faith, justice, truth, the family, the forces of darkness. *De nihilo nihilum, in nihilum nil posse reverti*, in a well-worn phrase dating back to Aristotle: nothing can come of nothing, nor can return to it. *King Lear* has been called Christian and anti-Christian, drawing on the books of Job and Revelation in its portrait of a man brought lower than any other in the canon — and a king, what's more, 'anointed flesh', with all hope of redemption brutally snatched away at the last. For all its apocalyptic scale, *Lear* is less about the divine order than man's suffering; for all its resonance about the human condition, it is about one reckless individual who had 'ever but slenderly known himself'. For all its unremitting bleakness, and the merciless blackout of its ending, it leaves behind a sense of affirmation.

By the time *Lear* was performed before King James at his Whitehall palace on 26 December 1606, it must already have been playing at the Globe most of that year, as Shakespeare's next play — an even darker, if less universal tragedy — had received its first performances that summer. Whatever the playwright thought James might make of *Lear*, *Macbeth* was much more overtly addressed to the monarch — a Scottish play, distorting history to pay tribute to his ancestry while thinking the unthinkable, uneasily topical: a successful attempt at regicide.

Late the previous year, on 5 November 1605, a Catholic plot to kill the King was foiled when conspirators were caught in the act of attempting to blow up the Palace of Westminster while James was opening the new session

(PAGES 238–239)
MACBETH AND THE THREE
WITCHES.
PAINTING BY
THEODORE CHASSERIAU,
1819–56.

of parliament. The true leader of the Gunpowder Plot, as it has become known to history – or the 'Powder Treason', as it was called at the time – was Robert Catesby of Warwickshire, son of that same Sir William Catesby known to Shakespeare's father, from whom he had probably obtained the Catholic Testament found hidden in the roof of Henley Street.

Shakespeare's recusant Warwickshire connections were perilously close to returning to cause him trouble. Names far more obscure than that of the sometime William Shakeshafte were ruthlessly tortured out of the conspirators before they were put to death. It is another index of how well Shakespeare covered his tracks, to the eternal despair of his biographers, that he did not merely survive this dangerous episode, but felt emboldened to work it into his next play – performed before the King in August 1606, during a visit from his brother-in-law, the King of Denmark.

Macbeth was riddled with references to the Powder Treason, only too clear to contemporary audiences. Its running theme of 'equivocation' made topical play of the Jesuit doctrine by which a prisoner under interrogation might in good conscience disguise the truth to avoid incriminating himself. James, moreover, believed in witchcraft. He took sorcery seriously enough to have written a treatise on the subject, *Daemonologie*, published in 1597. In August 1605, during a visit to Oxford, he had sat through an entertainment called *Tres Sybillae*, in which forerunners of Shakespeare's Three Witches loyally hailed his royal ancestry, then led a discussion of 'whether the imagination can produce real effects'.

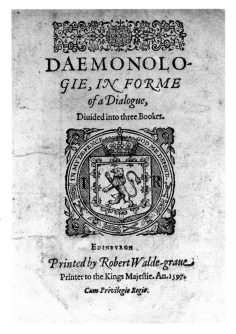

Does Macbeth, for instance, really see the witches, the dagger, Banquo's ghost? Of course he does, even if others don't. James certainly believed so; as James VI of Scotland, the son of an assassin's victim, he had been deeply disturbed by the discovery of a waxen image of himself, made with murderous intent by his mother's third husband, the Earl of Bothwell. But James was duly reassured when a witch declared him '*un homme de Dieu*'; if he had the devil's own word that he was under God's protection, then it must

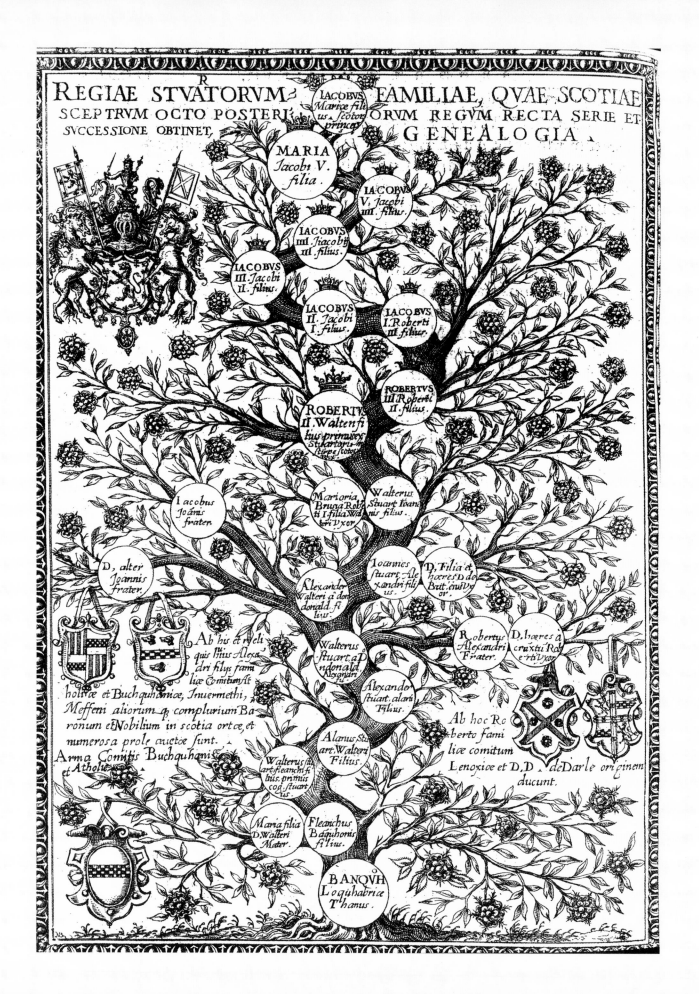

indeed be true. So the King would have approved of the notion of Macbeth's entanglement with the Weird Sisters. Such figures, to him, were no mere fantasies; they represented, as in Shakespeare's play, a central facet of man's permanent struggle against the powers of evil.

Whatever his private feelings (which appear to leave room for doubt), James also affected to believe in the ancient tradition, dating back to Edward the Confessor, of the power of the 'King's touch' to cure scrofula and other diseases. It handily buttressed another aspect of monarchy he was at pains to re-emphasise — the 'Divine Right' of English kings, chosen and anointed by God, thus rendering any attempt on their lives blasphemy as well as treason. For all his distaste at mingling with *hoi polloi*, let alone touching their running sores, he had recently revived the practice of 'touching' the afflicted, earning himself another polite nod from Shakespeare via Malcolm, exiled at the London court.

But the central tribute paid by the wary King's man to his employer was a wholesale rewriting of history to boost the Stuart ego. In Shakespeare's primary source, Holinshed's *Chronicles*, Duncan is a young and weak king murdered at Inverness by a group of conspirators including both Macbeth and Banquo. Shakespeare transforms Banquo from a murderous conspirator into an honourable martyr, engineering the escape of his son Fleance, much to Macbeth's anguish, to father a line of monarchs down to and including the very king sitting in the audience. James frequently said in public speeches that he hoped the House of Stuart would reign over Britain 'to the end of the world'; and the mirror carried by the last monarch in Act IV's 'Show of Kings' suggests as much: that the Stuart line, recently traced back to Banquo in Leslie's *De Origine Scotorum* (1578), would stretch from Fleance past James 'to th' crack of doom'.

The theme of sleep, or lack of it, becomes obsessive in *Macbeth*. Is it entirely idle to wonder if Shakespeare himself was suffering sleepless nights while writing it? Never in his adult life, as mightily productive as it had already been, had he poured so much of himself into four such ambitious and draining works. Lack of sleep would fit with the symptoms of the nervous illness about to overwhelm him.

(OPPOSITE)
GENEALOGICAL TREE SHOWING KING JAMES I'S DESCENT FROM BANQUO. FROM 'DE ORIGINE, MORIBUS ET REBUS GESTIS SCOTORUM LIBRI DECEM' BY JOHN LESLIE, 1578.

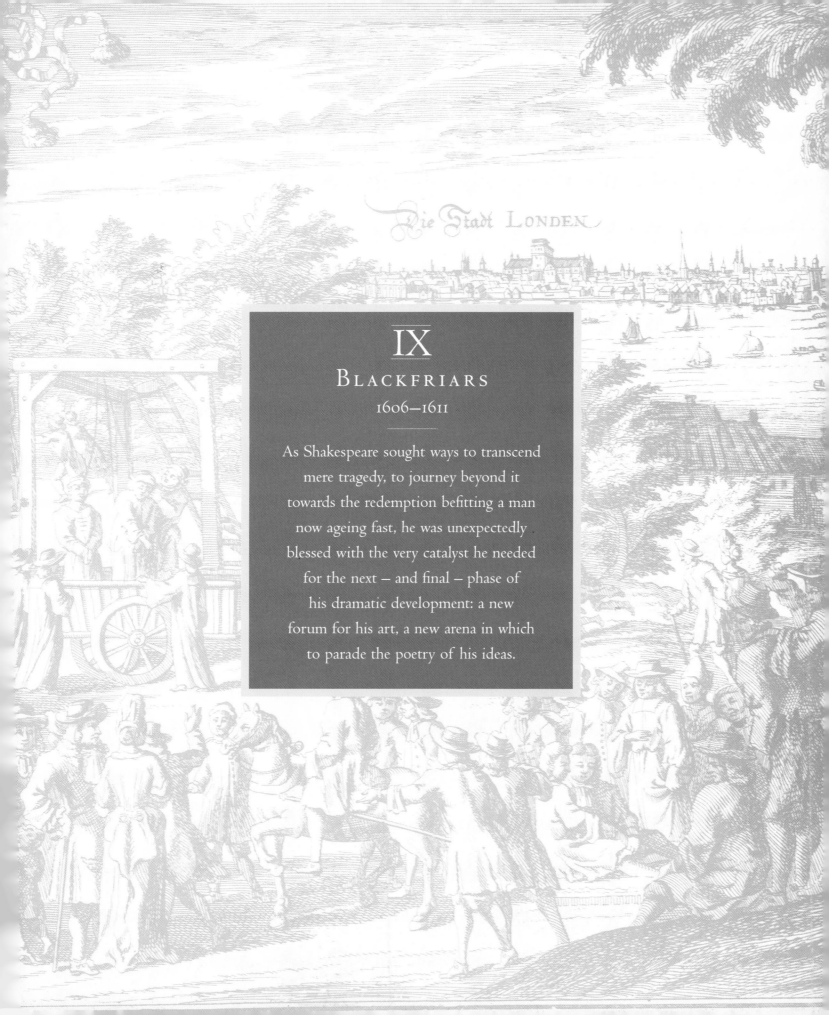

IX

BLACKFRIARS

1606–1611

As Shakespeare sought ways to transcend
mere tragedy, to journey beyond it
towards the redemption befitting a man
now ageing fast, he was unexpectedly
blessed with the very catalyst he needed
for the next — and final — phase of
his dramatic development: a new
forum for his art, a new arena in which
to parade the poetry of his ideas.

At the beginning of his professional career, Shakespeare would have taken four days to walk from Stratford to London, stopping overnight at Banbury, Oxford and Beaconsfield before proceeding down what is today the Uxbridge Road past Shepherd's Bush, on via Tyburn, dread scene of the gallows (now Marble Arch), past Westminster and Whitehall (seat of the government and court) to the city gate near Blackfriars. Even in later, more prosperous years, on horseback, he would always break his two-day ride at the same tavern in Oxford – then the Bull, later the Salutation, now the Crown, today hidden behind the inevitable McDonalds fast-food joint at No. 3 Cornmarket.

The landlord and his wife, John and Jeanette Davenant, were longstanding friends. During the 1590s they were London wine importers, based directly across the Thames from the Globe, where Shakespeare would first have met them. But these London years, although prosperous, were not happy ones for the Davenants. Jeanette bore John six children, all of whom died in infancy. Clearly desperate to try for more, the couple decided to leave the polluted capital and seek healthier climes upstream, moving their worldly goods by barge to Oxford in the new-start year of 1600. There, as if to prove a turn-of-the-seventeenth century ecological point, Jeanette Davenant proceeded to bear John no

UNATTRIBUTED
ENGRAVING OF SCENE AT
TYBURN SHOWING CROWDS
GATHERED TO WATCH
A HANGING, 1696.

(PAGE 244)
HEAD OF A MAN,
TRADITIONALLY CALLED
WILLIAM SLY,
ELIZABETHAN ACTOR.
ENGLISH SCHOOL,
SEVENTEENTH CENTURY.
(OPPOSITE)
THE DEATH OF CORDELIA,
FROM 'KING LEAR'.
PAINTING BY JOHANN
HEINRICH FÜSSLI,
1741–1825.

fewer than seven more children, all of whom survived into adulthood, ʀ
ripe old ages.

'A very beautiful woman,' according to Aubrey, 'of a very good ᴠ
of conversation extremely agreeable,' Jeanette was past thirty by the tⁱ
moved to Oxford, and a well-preserved thirty-seven when she bore hᴇ
child there, a second son, at the end of February 1606. That Shakespeare
to be William Davenant's godfather is a well-attested Oxford tradition; ᴍ
even a word-of-mouth account of the long-standing family friend hold
infant beside the font at his christening at the parish church
of St Martin Carfax, just down the road from the Bull, on
3 March. The boy was presumably named after his parents'
celebrated playwright friend. But was Shakespeare also his
natural father?

So Sir William Davenant, poet laureate, playwright
and impresario, himself liked to claim in later life, usually
in his cups, wassailing with cronies like the writer
Samuel Butler. 'When he was pleasant,' Aubrey continued,
'over a glass of wine with his most intimate friends, Sir
William would sometimes say that it seemed to him that
he writ with the very spirit that [did] Shakespeare, and was
contented enough to be thought his Son …' The author of
significant works ranging from revenge tragedies (such as
Albovine) to tragicomedies (*The Colonel and The Witts*), and
volumes of lyric poetry (*Madagascar*) to epic verse
(*Gondibert*), Davenant maintained a swaggering, man-about-
town persona despite the unsightly loss of his nose to the
mercury treatment then in common use for syphilis.

He was an engaging rogue, whose boast may have been no more
wishful thinking. But four centuries of detective work have failed to dis
it, only adding to the tantalising evidence. Certainly, Shakespeare stayed
Davenant's parents in Oxford as a close friend of the family, dating baᴄ
their London days, rather than as a paying guest. In 1698, with heavy innuᴇ
Charles Gildon noted that Shakespeare often stayed at the Davenant taᵛ

l. Greenhill pinx.

$\mathcal{S}$. G

(OPPOSITE)
CHARMIAN AND THE
SOOTHSAYER. FROM
'ANTONY AND
CLEOPATRA'.
PAINTING BY
MATTHEW WILLIAM
PETERS,
1742–1814.

Uɴ
S

THE
KINGDOME
OF
ENGLAND

SCOTLAND

PART OF IRE: LAND

THE IRISH SEA

MAN ISLE

ANGLESEY

Dublyn

County Wexford

A Lady.

A Gentleman.

A Citizens wife.

A Countryman.

Iodocus Hondius Flander.
celavit: Anno Dom. 1610.

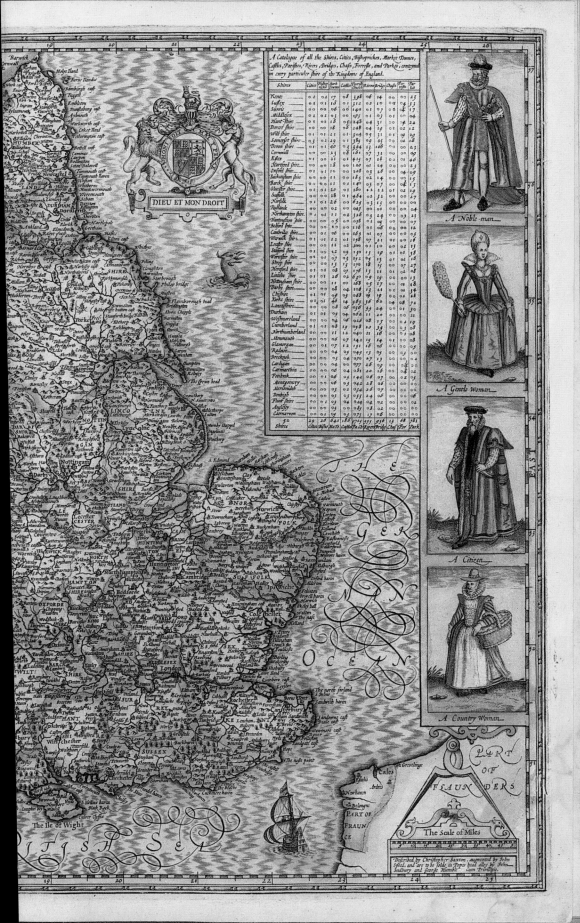

Map of England, from 'Theatrum Imperii Magnae Britanniae', by John Speed, 1616.

'whether for the beautiful mistress of the house, or the good wine, I shall not determine.' By 1709 the rumours about Davenant's parentage had been noted as 'an Oxford tradition' by a source as unimpeachable as a keeper of the Bodleian Library, Thomas Hearne, also a respected local antiquary. Shakespeare was Davenant's godfather and 'gave him his name,' recorded Hearne, who could not resist adding parenthetically: 'In all probability he got him.'

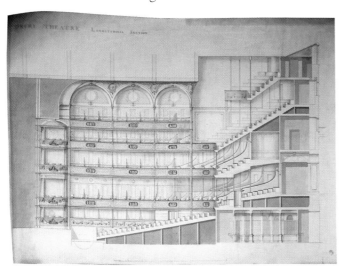

DRURY LANE THEATRE. SECTIONAL DRAWING OF THE INTERIOR BY HENRY HOLLAND, 1745–1806.

Whatever the truth, Davenant turned out to be a son – or perhaps merely a godson – in whom Shakespeare would have been well pleased. In 1656, forty years after the poet's death, the first attempt to revive drama since the Puritan prohibition was made by Sir William Davenant, who successfully petitioned King Charles II for the right of 'making fit' nine Shakespeare plays; he himself 'reformed' *Macbeth* and *The Tempest*, the latter in partnership with John Dryden, who praised Davenant as 'a man of quick and piercing imagination'. A tireless and versatile man of letters, Ben Jonson's successor in 1638 as poet laureate, Davenant was one of those prominent writers not afraid of political risks. Knighted in 1643 by Charles I for running supplies across the English Channel, he was thrown in the Tower eleven years later for espousing the Stuart cause in its Parisian exile, carrying messages between the King and Queen, and attempting to help embattled American royalists. He languished in the Tower for two years, 'pretty certain that I shall be hanged next week'; it is said that 'Milton saved him from execution and that ten years later Davenant was able to return the favour'. By the time of his death in 1668, he had reinvented himself as a dramatist, theatre manager and producer, founding such celebrated London theatres as Covent Garden and Drury Lane. In the process, he also introduced female actors to the English stage.

(OPPOSITE)
MACBETH AND THE
THREE WITCHES.
PAINTING BY
JOHN WOTTON,
1686–1765.

Over the ensuing centuries, the beauty of Jeanette Davenant has contin-ued to exercise a fascination over fusty Shakespeare scholars which they cannot, however reluctantly, quite bring themselves to relinquish. Shaw is not alone in naming Jeanette as his candidate for the 'Dark Lady' of the Sonnets, who seems to have caused Shakespeare such paroxysms of jealousy. Given the date of her son William's birth — and the possibility that he was the product of an extended liaison, more than merely a one-night stand — Jeanette may in fact have been a spur to the creation of Shakespeare's Desdemona, moving him to Othello-like agonies as he rode on to Stratford or London next morning, leav-ing her to return to her husband's bed.

Nine months before William Davenant's birth, Shakespeare would have been finishing *Macbeth* — with his next work, as was his wont, already taking shape in his head. Cleopatra, according to Shakespeare's copy of North's Plutarch, was thirty-eight years old when her tempestuous fling with Mark Antony ended in her suicide — exactly the same age as Jeanette Davenant while Shakespeare was writing *Antony and Cleopatra*. Shakespeare himself was forty-three, some ten years younger than Antony. Was it pure coincidence, if he was bedding the wife of the Oxford tavern-keeper, that he now chose to conjure up — through the besotted eyes of an older man — the most alluring, highly sexed woman ever to emerge even from his capacious and libidinous imagina-tion, a woman for whom her lover would surrender 'half the bulk o' th' world', a woman whom age could not wither, 'nor custom stale her infinite variety'?

Hercules at the Crossroads: the hero forced to choose between the paths of Pleasure and Virtue might as well have been Shakespeare himself, reluctant to leave the pleasures of Oxford for the virtuous roads north or south. It is also Mark Antony, abandoning his responsibilities in Rome for a voluptuous dalliance in Egypt.

As Julius Caesar was informed by the external events of the moment, so its sequel seems to derive its unique richness and vitality from Shakespeare's own internal life at the time. In the wake of *Othello*, *Lear* and *Macbeth* he was riding a mighty creative wave, intent on only the broadest of horizons; if he was also enjoying a dangerous love affair in Oxford, spiced with guilt about his

(OPPOSITE)
CORDELIA COMFORTING
HER FATHER, KING LEAR,
IN PRISON, 1886.
PAINTING BY
GEORGE WILLIAM JOY,
1844–1925.

domestic responsibilities, the synchronicity moved him to some of his boldest, most bravura writing. The 'happy valiancy' (in Coleridge's phrase) with which the play flits dizzily from place to place, often empires apart, causes none of the traditional problems to this century of cinema; it may also mirror Shakespeare's own, unwonted sense of dislocation if he were riding up and down the Oxford road — sometimes without proceeding on to Stratford — rather more often than usual.

Antony and Cleopatra did not appear in print before the First Folio of 1623. It was entered in the Stationers Register by the printer Edward Blount on 20 May 1608, but perhaps merely as a 'blocking entry', a device to deter pirates, for it seems to have remained unpublished. He had perhaps had it in mind to return to North's Plutarch since drawing on its Life of Marcus Antonius for *Julius Caesar* seven years earlier. The action of *Antony and Cleopatra* opens in 40 BC, two years after the end of the earlier play, and covers (if imperceptibly) a period of ten years. Antony himself is distinctly older, though his rival Octavius remains, with dramatic licence, 'scarce-bearded'. These and other central characters are built largely on Plutarch's own shrewd foundations, but such distinctive figures as Antony's right-hand man, Enobarbus, and Cleopatra's handmaidens, Charmian and Iras, are Shakespeare's own creatures.

He would also have known versions of the story in Horace, Virgil, Spenser and Tasso, but Shakespeare makes this doomed coupling very much his own. There is a strong sense of predestination throughout the play, as if both these mighty public figures were playing out aspects of human frailty en route to an inevitable personal tragedy. Rarely did even he so powerfully intertwine the global and the domestic.

The historical Mark Antony did not commit suicide on the same day as Cleopatra — nor so soon after his defeat at Actium as Shakespeare, for obvious dramatic reasons, suggests. In Plutarch's account, the disillusioned Antony 'forsook the city and company of his friends, and built himself a house in the sea by the Isle of Pharos … and dwelt there, as a man that banished himself from all men's company: saying that he would lead Timon's life, because he had the like wrong offered him, that was before offered unto Timon: and that for the unthankfulness of those he had done good unto, and whom he took to be

(OPPOSITE)
ROMEO AND JULIET, 1884.
PAINTING BY
SIR FRANK DICKSEE,
1853–1928.

his friends, he was angry with all men, and would trust no man.'

Rather than forfeit his compact, ineluctable ending to *Antony and Cleopatra*, Shakespeare chose to pick up on Plutarch's mention of Timon of Athens, and convert this episode into a play bearing his name. His longstanding interest in the dangerous properties of money, and the complexities of money-lending, returned to supply a motive – nowhere mentioned in Plutarch – for Timon's disenchantment with his fellow countrymen. Were the begging letters still arriving from Stratford? Had the borough applied to Shakespeare for financial assistance, having offered none to his father in his hour of need? So felt is the fury Shakespeare gave Timon that it is tempting to look for external events which might have had the poet himself in misanthropic mode, railing at the world and all its works as his own life took unwelcome turns for the worse. But this is a period of which we know little, and can assume less, beyond his satisfaction in the marriage of his twenty-four-year-old daughter Susanna to the estimable Stratford physician, Dr John Hall, on 5 June 1607.

Was Shakespeare ready to 'turn his back on London', like Timon on Athens? Not yet. Late payments, both as debtor and creditor, continued to plague his creative peace of mind, but he was otherwise at his most ferociously productive. In an age of usury, whose capacity for evil had touched his own life – 'for loan oft loses both itself and friend' – Shakespeare perhaps saw himself offering his own Olympian brand of fashionably topical satire in *Timon*; for, as this new burst of Roman plays took to the stage between 1606 and 1608, Ben Jonson was giving the King's Men some of his most powerful, of-the-moment satires in *Volpone* and *The Alchemist*.

But Shakespeare had the Roman bit securely between his teeth. In Timon he had created an archetype of what have been called his 'minimized' heroes – those tragic figures with whom he does not seem to require his audience to sympathise or engage to any great degree of fellow-feeling. Now he would achieve the supreme example of this 'marginalized' man, the great-hearted public figure 'incapable of adjusting himself to society', in Coriolanus.

In January 1608, during the coldest winter London had known since 1565, fires were lit along the frozen Thames. The previous year had seen riots around the Midlands over rising food prices; ever fearful of mobs, especially unruly

(PAGES 258–259)
CORIOLANUS WITH HIS
WIFE AND MOTHER.
FRENCH SCHOOL,
SEVENTEENTH CENTURY.
(OPPOSITE)
OTHELLO,
THE MOOR OF VENICE,
1826.
PAINTING BY
JAMES NORTHCOTE,
1746–1831.

ones, James had issued a proclamation deploring the 'notorious' development that 'many of the meanest sort of our people have presumed lately to assemble themselves riotously in multitudes'. Shakespeare himself, still hoarding grain in those barns at New Place, kept one commercial eye on the main chance while turning another blazing one on the incompetence of witless aristocrats-turned-politicians.

Snobs like Coriolanus, observed Wyndham Lewis, must have 'pullulated' in the courts of Elizabeth and James – overgrown schoolboys with 'crazed' notions of privilege and a 'demented' ideal of authority. That Shakespeare despised them is clear throughout his work. But where once, as in the history plays, he filled their mouths with pompous rhetoric, he is now intent upon their enlightenment, their alteration, perhaps even their salvation.

While writing *Coriolanus*, a supreme master of his craft long rid of any youthful insecurities, Shakespeare would have been feeling some nostalgia for his early years in London as an aspirant poet. In Volumnia, for sure, he was in part paying a discreet private homage to the late Queen. But the events he was now dramatising followed hard upon those he had addressed fifteen years earlier in *The Rape of Lucrece*. Fifth-century Rome was a very different place after the expulsion of the monarchy; now, with all the fellow-feeling his protagonist lacks, Shakespeare can expand the role of the Tribunes to shape the nearest he ever came to a statement of his own political views, in its way an essay on class and democracy, very much on the side of the common man, the fickle, wilful but 'poor, bare, fork'd' animal – as yet an unruly mob, as much in need of civic education as their aristocratic overlords.

As if for that purpose, he seems suddenly to create yet another new language, entirely his own: harsh, austere, driven, at times comic, at times angry, always in deadly earnest. With *Coriolanus*, as with *Lear*, we can almost hear Shakespeare inventing the English language as we have inherited it, driving each syllable forward from its crude, rough-edged origins to a range and eloquence we owe solely to him. Philosophically, meanwhile, he shows himself capable yet again of arguing an empirical case, this time a political one, in terms of the most profound humanity. As Shakespeare again weighs personal failings against national destiny, his inflexible hero at the last shows a tenderness which might, had it emerged earlier, have been the making of him; as it is, he does so knowing that it will prove dangerous to him, if not 'most mortal'. Redemption, of a kind, was already playing around the edges of the poet's mind. Soon it would take centre-stage.

Antony, Timon, Coriolanus: mighty, larger-than-life men, but all deeply flawed, to a sufficient extent to discourage the natural sympathy we have felt for such recent tragic heroes as Hamlet, Othello, Lear, Macbeth. Shakespeare has travelled far indeed since Titus, Romeo, Shylock and Falstaff. The portraits on the walls of his imagination are steadily growing, if not larger and deeper, ever closer to home. Of late he had taken to inhabiting his own plays more directly, more unsettlingly than ever. Soon the strain would inevitably tell.

DRAWING OF BLACKFRIARS THEATRE, C.1650.
UNKNOWN ARTIST.

But the unavoidable consequence of these outpourings, tightly controlled as they were, would coincide with an important new era in the life of the King's Men. As Shakespeare sought ways to transcend mere tragedy, to journey beyond it towards the redemption befitting a man now ageing fast, he was unexpectedly blessed with the very catalyst he needed for the next – and final – phase of his dramatic development: a new forum for his art, a new arena in which to parade the poetry of his ideas. A new theatre, in short – smaller, with room for only some 700 spectators paying higher prices, for all were seated. And protected from the elements. The Blackfriars theatre had a roof.

Writing for an indoor theatre, lit by candles, would wring from Shakespeare one last, great burst of creative innovation, the startling but logical culmination of all that had gone before. At the same time, it meant that the King's Men could more than double their business, running a winter season at the Blackfriars on top of their summer afternoons at the Globe. As a major shareholder, he would have played a significant part in the ambitious decision

to take over the lease of the Blackfriars from Henry Evans, the Welsh scrivener-turned-impresario whose 'little eyases' had caused Hamlet and the King's Men such grief at the turn of the century.

Nine years later, after a prosperous decade courting the kind of controversy which did the box-office no harm, they had finally gone too far. Those local worthies who had not wanted the Lord Chamberlain's Men in their back yard were now only too happy to welcome the King's Men after a series of unwelcome alarums. The last straw was the royal displeasure occasioned by the boy-actors' 1608 production of *The Conspiracy and Tragedy of Charles, Duke of Byron*. Its caricature of the King of France so outraged the French ambassador that King James himself felt obliged to close them down. So Evans — already the subject of lurid tales concerning his 'press-ganging' of reluctant children — was in no position to drive a hard bargain with the Burbages over his lease, which they secured for a mere £40 a year. It was shared between a seven-strong syndicate including Shakespeare.

The Blackfriars agreement was signed on 9 August 1608. Within a week one of the seven new joint-lessees (or 'housekeepers'), an actor named William Sly, dropped dead. Along with Heminges, Condell, the Burbage brothers and a mysterious investor named Thomas Evans, Shakespeare now owned one-sixth of the business. It had cost him £5 14s 4d; and it would eventually prove many more times as lucrative than his one-sixteenth share of the Globe. By 1636, twenty years after his death, Shakespeare's heirs would be receiving £90 a year from the Blackfriars as compared with £25 from the Globe.

As shrewd as ever with his money, one eye already fixed on his daughters' inheritance, Shakespeare did not warm to the Blackfriars for the pecuniary gain so much as the new dramatic opportunities it offered. As much as he owed the groundlings, for whose rudimentary tastes he had contentedly catered all these years, he could now bid them a fond farewell and concentrate solely on the more refined, profound level beneath all those 'two-tier' plays since *As You Like It*. By accident or design, *Coriolanus* became an appropriate adieu, complete with cautionary warning, to the 1d playgoers who liked their humour broad, their heroes princely and their action bloody. Now he could charge 6d, and rein himself in to the sublime.

In his mid-forties, after some thirty-two plays, Shakespeare's powers of invention were clearly as fresh as ever. But shifts in creative direction tend to be dictated as much by internal as external events. Over the last four years he had put himself under tremendous strain; if his private life had remained adventurous, if indeed he had suffered the stress of an eventful extra-marital affair, he had also produced three of his mightiest tragedies, moving straight on to the two Roman plays generally held to be quite comparable achievements. Business activities and political events, with all the complexities of life at court, would also have taken their toll.

If *Timon* marked a tighter focus, perhaps showing signs of tiredness, *Pericles* would see Shakespeare entering a whole new world of the imagination, where the once dark powers of the supernatural become a shining force for good, wringing miraculous deliveries from apparent disasters, finding pots of philosophical gold at the end of distinctly dubious rainbows. From *Timon* to

VIEW FROM SOUTHWARK. ENGRAVING BY NATHANIEL WHITTOCK AFTER ANTHONY VAN WYNDGAERDEN, 1543.

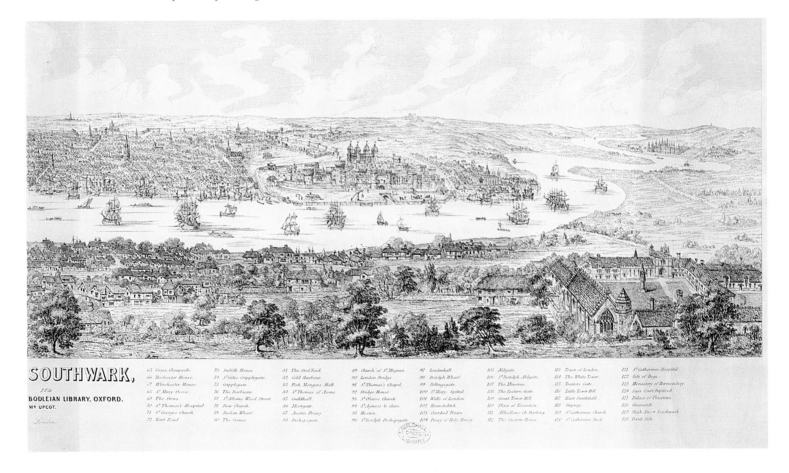

SOUTHWARK,

BODLEIAN LIBRARY, OXFORD.
MR UPCOT.

Pericles is a giant conceptual leap. Although the two plays appear to have been written in the same year, 1607–08, it is impossible not to believe that something happened in between, something in Shakespeare's offstage life to change the tint in his window on the world.

It was a period of domestic woes – and joys – both in Stratford and in London. In the last week of 1607, his brother Edmund died at the age of only twenty-seven. A jobbing actor of no particular renown, the only member of the family to have followed William into the theatre, Edmund was buried on New Year's Eve in the church of St Mary Overy, Southwark (now Southwark Cathedral), within a bell's toll of the Globe. Brothers Gilbert and Richard would presumably have come down from Stratford to join William for the occasion, the three older brothers representing their elderly mother in mourning the youngest.

It seems that Edmund had only recently smiled in the direction of his namesake in *King Lear* by fathering an illegitimate son of his own, who died in infancy. The entry for 12 August 1607 in the register for St Giles Church without Cripplegate reads: 'Edward, son of Edward Shackspeere, player, base-born.' The clerk who wrote 'Edward' for 'Edmund' also wrote Joan for Joanna, Eleanor for Helen, Orton for Horton, Morgan for Martin. Someone 'of means', as has rightly been pointed out, must have paid for Edmund's curiously lavish funeral four months later, which involved a 'rather large' burial fee on top of that for 'a forenoon knell of the great bell'. If this someone was his prosperous brother, as surely it was, the 'forenoon' tolling of that bell would indicate a midday funeral, enabling the bereaved and his fellow-actors to return to the theatre in time for their afternoon performance.

The following February, as he approached his forty-fourth birthday, Shakespeare meanwhile became a grandfather. Only eight months after marrying Dr. John Hall, Susanna bore him a daughter, baptised with the name Elizabeth in Stratford on 21 February. Like father, like daughter; Susanna herself had been born six months after her parents' hasty ('o'erhasty'?) marriage. 'Witty above her sex', according to her epitaph, and 'wise to salvation', the feisty Susanna may have taken after her father in other ways, too. In May 1606 her name was listed among those who had broken the law by fail-

(OPPOSITE)
DESDEMONA, FROM
'OTHELLO'
PAINTING BY
FREDERIC LEIGHTON,
1830–96.

ing to receive the Sacrament the previous Easter. She did not turn up in court on the due date for her appearance, but the charge was eventually dismissed.

Whatever her feelings about two generations of offspring born out of wedlock, Mary Arden lived to see the birth of her first great-grandchild. But on 9 September Shakespeare was back at Holy Trinity to bury his mother, dead at the age of sixty-eight. Amid all this unwonted activity he still found time to pursue his debtors, that August suing John Addenbrooke for the recovery of £6, plus 24s damages, in a Court of Record case that would drag on till the following June. By then he would be distracted by the worst example yet of pirate publication, while writing a play yet further sanctifying daughters.

Shipwrecks, riddles, resurrections: Shakespeare is palpably excited to have found a brave new imaginary world to explore, new themes consonant with his altered mood, mellow, reflective, forgiving. In *Pericles* he can begin to see his route towards *The Tempest*, the natural end of the long intellectual road he had travelled. It marks the start of a clear course towards his apparent farewell, laying the foundations of the great triptych which would draw all his work together towards a logical, contemplative, serene conclusion.

The evident alteration in Shakespeare, and the slow burn towards the exhilaration with which he rises to this last plateau, upon which his poetry reaches its most exalted, inexorably combine to signify some radical occurrence during 1608. The influential Victorian critic Edward Dowden found in the calmness and maturity of Shakespeare's last plays evidence of his emergence from 'the depths of despair'; the poet's final work proceeded from 'an elderly serenity, a marvellous rural detachment, a hard-won peace.' Similar thoughts beset the magisterial E.K. Chambers, fifty years later in the early 1920s, to the point where even this most sober of Bardographers felt moved to speculate that the poet had suffered 'a serious illness', perhaps even 'a nervous break-down'.

During 1609 a printer named Thomas Thorpe published 154 of Shakespeare's Sonnets, which had been circulating privately since he first wrote them while in Southampton's household some ten years before. Also in the volume was a mannered, 329-line poem in seven-line 'rhyme royal' stanzas enti-tled 'A Lover's Complaint', which seems highly unlikely to be even the young

Shakespeare's work; but the Sonnets certainly were. Unlike *Venus and Adonis* and *The Rape of Lucrece*, whose publication Shakespeare had personally overseen, the Sonnets were riddled with misprints, arranged in suspect order, and prefaced on the second leaf of the quarto by an ornate inscription which has since caused as much trouble as the riddle of the Sphinx:

TO.THE.ONLY.BEGETTER.OF.

THESE.ENSUING.SONNETS.

Mr.W.H. ALL.HAPPINESS.

AND.THAT.ETERNITY.

PROMISED.

BY.

OUR.EVER-LIVING.POET.

WISHETH.

THE.WELL-WISHING.

ADVENTURER.IN.

SETTING.

FORTH.

T.T.

The plain, inescapable fact is that, whatever the dedication may mean, and whatever the identity of its dedicatee, it was written and signed not by Shakespeare himself but by the piratical printer, Thomas Thorpe. Mr W.H. is not the 'fair youth', but the man who procured a set of the Sonnets and handed them over to Thorpe – who is now, dutifully if over-elaborately, thanking him.

Candidates for *this* Mr W.H., the unscrupulous rogue who slipped the Sonnets to a buccaneer printer – probably for a slice of the proceeds, and probably knowing full well that Shakespeare regarded them as private, to be circulated only among friends – have been almost as numerous as candidates for the Mr W.H. who never existed, the Mr. W.H. wrongly identified as the 'fair youth' to whom they are addressed. Contenders for both roles have ranged from Henry Wriothesley, Earl of Southampton (with his initials craftily reversed to avoid detection); William Herbert, Earl of Pembroke, a respectable

enough patron and admirer to be Heminges' and Condell's choice as the co-dedicatee of the First Folio; and Sir William Hervey, third husband of Southampton's mother. Hervey is the hot favourite to be Thorpe's supplier because, as soon as his wife died in 1608, he published a 'poetical testament' which she had deemed 'too intimate' to share with the public; the 'eternity promised by our ever-living poet' has been explained in terms of Harvey's remarriage, the following year, to a much younger wife, Cordelia Annesley. But why would any of these titled noblemen be addressed by a social inferior as plain 'Mr'?

Beyond these usual suspects, leading contenders have included the stationer William Hall, whose name leaps out from the dedication by removing the third point in 'Mr. W.H.ALL'. Then there is William Hatcliffe, Prince of Purpoole (Lord of Misrule) at the Grays Inn Christmas revels of 1587–88. Great energy has been devoted to the unlikely hypothesis that this once golden youth, now an obscure Lincolnshire lawyer dogged by debt, travelled to London twenty years later to flog his set of the Sonnets to Thomas Thorpe. Just as valid is the engagingly dotty theory of the German scholar D. Barnstorff that Mr. W.H. was none other than 'Master William Himself', a boon to those who believe the poet addressed his Sonnets to himself, but on a par with Professor Donald Foster's wishful thinking – pinning the rap, yet again, on the hard-working, long-suffering compositors – that 'Mr W.H.' is a misprint for 'Mr W. Sh.' No, perhaps the most likely thief of the Sonnets – a distinctly non-literary figure into whose hands they could easily have fallen, and whose life was one long litany of debt litigation – was in fact much closer to home: Shakespeare's indigent brother-in-law, William Hathaway.

With a more sophisticated audience, and no unruly groundlings to disrupt proceedings, Shakespeare could write much more intimate scenes for the indoor Blackfriars theatre than for the roofless playhouses. In the second act of *Cymbeline*, the villainous Iachimo tiptoes around the sleeping Imogen's chamber, where he has been hiding in a trunk. By the light of a single taper, he notes down the room's contents: the paintings, the window, the bedclothes, the pictures on the arras. Then he leans over the sleeping girl herself, notes the

(PAGES 272–273)
MACBETH.
PAINTING BY
JOSEPH ANTON KOCH
VON GEMÄLDE,
1768–1839.

mole on her left breast, the title of the book left open on her bedside table, removes her bracelet, is even tempted to kiss her.

The terrifying beauty of this scene had Simon Forman holding his breath when he saw *Cymbeline* in April 1611, six months before his death. 'Remember,' he recorded in his notebook, 'in the deepest of that night, she being asleep, he opened the chest and came forth of it, and viewed her in her bed, and the marks of her body; and took away her bracelet.' The scene would be just as effective, of course, during the play's seasonal transfer to the Globe (where Forman may, indeed, have seen it); the point is that, before the Blackfriars, Shakespeare might not have been minded to write it.

Marianne Moore wanted poets to be 'literalists of the imagination', presenting for inspection 'imaginary gardens with real toads in them'. There can be few more apt descriptions for the poetic landscape of Shakespeare's final romances, even before he anticipated her all too literally by presenting an imaginary seashore (if in a landlocked country) prowled by a real bear.

The most celebrated stage direction in theatrical history — 'Exit pursued by bear' — comes on the threshold from tragedy to redemption in his next play, carefully (for once) entitled *The Winter's Tale* — a phrase analagous since the mid-sixteenth-century with what was even then called an 'old wives' tale', thus readying his audience for a story of romantic improbability, to be marvelled at rather than taken at face value. Two separate characters in the last act of *The Winter's Tale* liken its events to those of 'an old tale', while it is the latest reincarnation of Hamnet, poor young Mamillius, who is made to remind us before he dies that 'a sad tale's best for winter'. Poignantly for the playwright — or by way, perhaps, of artful self-torture — the boy-actor playing Mamillius would later be resurrected as his lost-presumed-dead sister, Perdita.

Perdita is a young woman as idealised as Marina and Imogen, if not more so, in a direct line of ascent from Cordelia and beyond, distributing flowers

SHAKESPEARE'S SIGNATURE C.1610.

with all the abandon of a happier Ophelia. Shakespeare's preoccupation with his daughters, amid his continued mourning for his lost son, sees this latest paragon a true child of nature, rejoicing in her natural surroundings, rejecting anything as unnatural as cosmetics, flirting with egalitarianism (despite her own unknown royal birth), and having her worst fears confirmed when her lover's royal father angrily refuses to accept a mere shepherdess as his daughter-in-law.

The Winter's Tale was not published before the First Folio, where it appears as the last of the comedies. Simon Forman's diary tells us that he saw it at the Globe on 15 May 1611. In November of that year the account book of the Office of the Revels records a performance at court by the King's Men of 'Ye Winters night Tayle'. A 'philosopher of roguery', like Falstaff, Autolycus was Shakespeare's own brainchild, as were the pivotal characters of Leontes' steward Antigonus and his formidable wife Paulina. Otherwise, he is indeed dramatising an 'old tale', dating from 1588 — and an ironic choice, too, in *Pandosto: The Triumph of Time* (later retitled *Dorsastus and Fawnia*) by his old enemy Robert Greene. What better farewell to the London stage — the first of several, as it transpired, no doubt further irritating the 'university wits' — than a seigneurial improvement on the work of the man who had so scornfully greeted his arrival in the capital?

Retirement was already beckoning. As was the Warwickshire countryside, rarely celebrated with such lavish affection as in those flowers Proserpina is 'frighted' of letting fall from Dis's wagon. If Shakespeare had never particularly missed his wife, he seems to indulge in some wishful thinking about the marriage he never had via the old shepherd's moist-eyed Whitsun memories of his own, and her gift for hospitality. Was he offering Anne an oblique apology, trying in his long-distance way to atone for his own inadequacies as a husband and father? As he wrote plays yearning for reconciliation, not least between parents and their children, Shakespeare was more than ready to leave London, even to quit writing, and return to his roots, to the bosom of the growing family he had so long neglected. If he was going to bid the stage farewell, however, he was intent on doing so with one final, philosophical yet highly theatrical, flourish.

(OPPOSITE)
CYMBELINE, KING OF THE SOUTH-EAST OF ENGLAND, C.1809.
PAINTING BY GEORGE DAWE, 1781–1829.

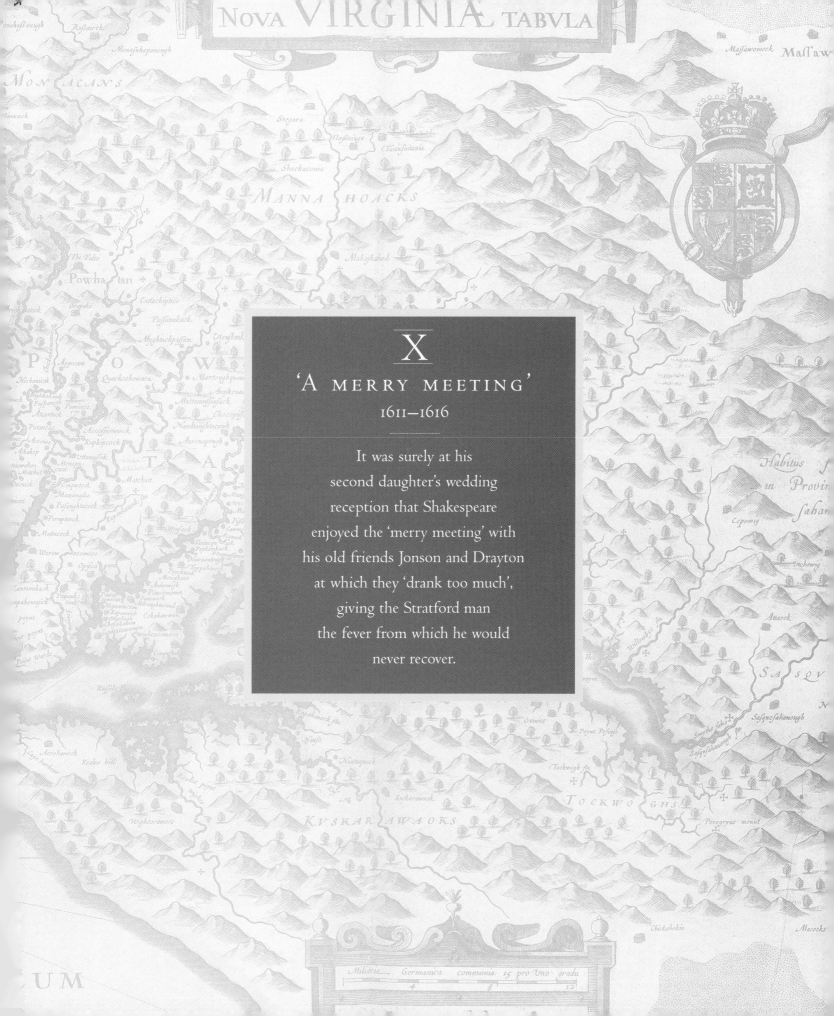

X

'A MERRY MEETING'
1611–1616

It was surely at his
second daughter's wedding
reception that Shakespeare
enjoyed the 'merry meeting' with
his old friends Jonson and Drayton
at which they 'drank too much',
giving the Stratford man
the fever from which he would
never recover.

On 24 July 1609 a sudden storm at sea broke up a small fleet of ships belonging to the Virginia Company which had set sail from Plymouth on 2 June. All eventually managed to arrive at Jamestown the following month, with the sole exception of the flagship, the *Sea Adventure*, carrying the admiral, Sir George Somers, and the future governor of Virginia, Sir Thomas Gates. Both men, along with all hands, were assumed to have perished.

Nine months later, on 23 May 1610, to the astonishment of the colonists, two small craft arrived at Jamestown carrying the full complement of the *Sea Adventure*. Somers and his crew, it transpired, had run aground on the island of Bermuda — a dread name to mariners then as now, for modern legends about the perils of the 'Bermuda Triangle' seem to have grown directly from the island's reputation in Elizabethan times as 'the Isle of Devils', where dire practices including cannibalism awaited visitors. But the stalwarts of the Virginia Company had encountered no such dark mysteries. On the contrary, they reported, they found Bermuda and its climate delightful, rich in food and shelter, with enough wood to build the small pinnaces in which they eventually completed their voyage to the New World.

Their story provoked enormous interest, both in Virginia and back home in England. One of the crew, Sylvester Jourdan, wrote an account published in pamphlet form as *A Discovery of the Bermudas, Otherwise Called the Isle of Devils*. The Virginia Company soon replied with its own version entitled *The True Declaration of the Estate of the Colony in Virginia, with a confutation of such scandalous reports as have tended to the disgrace of so worthy an enterprise*. And a further report, by William Strachey of the *Sea Adventure*, circulated in the form of a letter; entitled *The True Reportory of the Wrack and Redemption of Sir Thomas Gates*, it was dated 15 July 1610 (and eventually published in *Purchas His Pilgrims* in 1625).

Between them, these dramatic contemporary documents gave Shakespeare his framework for *The Tempest*, in which he blends his own responses to Montaigne with the recent adventures of the Virginia Company's crew to

A

DISCOVERY

OF THE BARMV

DAS, OTHERWISE

called the Ile of

DIVELS:

By Sir THOMAS GATES, Sir
GEORGE SOMMERS, and Cap-
tayne NEWPORT, with
diuers others.

Set forth for the loue of my Coun
try, and also for the good of the
Plantation in Virginia.

SIL. IOVRDAN.

LONDON,
Printed by *Iohn Windet*, and are to be sold by *Roger Barnes*
in S. *Dunstanes* Church-yard in Fleet-streete, vn-
der the Diall. 1610.

TITLE PAGE OF SYLVESTER JOURDAN'S
'A DISCOVERY OF THE BERMUDAS',
ONE OF SHAKESPEARE'S SOURCES FOR
'THE TEMPEST'.

(PAGE 278)
JOHN FLETCHER, C.1620.
AFTER UNKNOWN ARTIST.
(OPPOSITE)
TITLE PAGE OF 'MARINERS
MIRROUR', 1588.

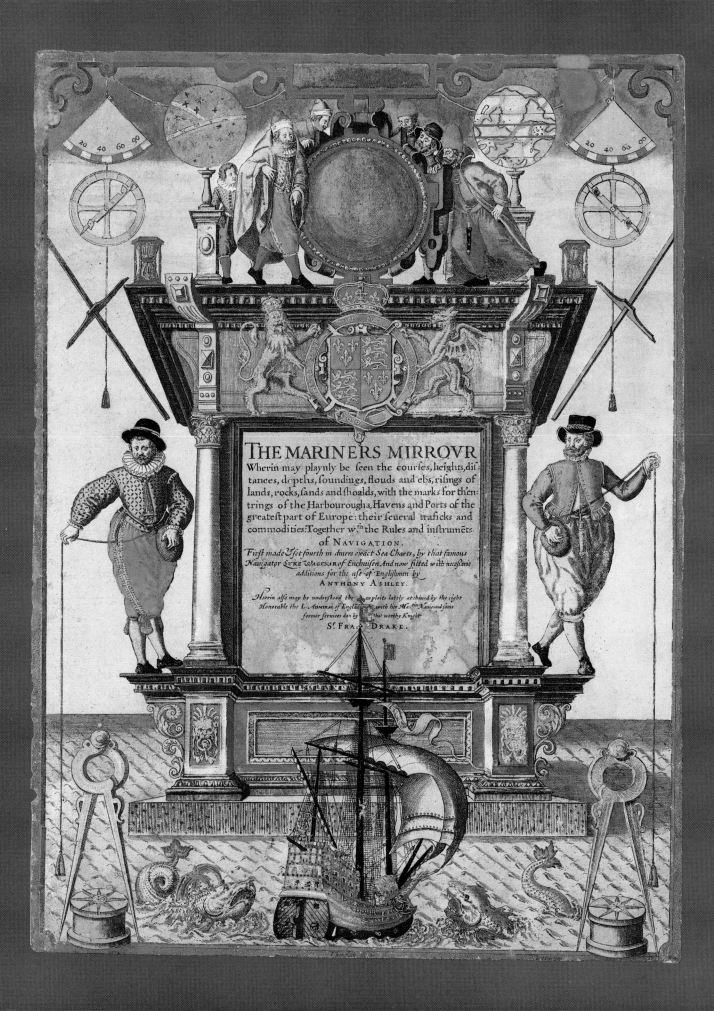

THE MARINERS MIRROVR

Wherin may playnly be seen the courses, heights, dis-
tances, depths, soundings, flouds and ebs, risings of
lands, rocks, sands and shoalds, with the marks for th'en-
trings of the Harbouroughs, Havens and Ports of the
greatest part of Europe: their seueral traficks and
commodities: Together w.th the Rules and instrumēts
of NAVIGATION.
First made & set fourth in diuers exact Sea-Charts, by that famous
Nauigator LVKE WAGENAR of Enchuisen And now fitted with necessarie
additions for the use of Englishmen by
ANTHONY ASHLEY.

Heerin also may be understood the exploits lately achiued by the right
Honorable the L. Admirai of Englād, with her Ma.tie Nauieand some
former seruices don by that worthy Knight
S.t FRA.s DRAKE.

THE
HISTORY OF
THE WORLD.

In Fiue Bookes.

Title page from Raleigh's
'History of the World', 1614.

create a fantasy island rooted in the Old World, placeless if distinctly Mediterranean, but part-peopled by the New. Thanks to another shipwreck, its indigenous 'New World' inhabitants have come under the natural command of the ousted Duke Prospero of Milan, whose 'art' (or what we would now call 'science') is pitched against the complex Elizabethan concept of 'nature' – a theme already explored in *King Lear* and *The Tempest*'s immediate predecessors, *Cymbeline* and *The Winter's Tale*.

Are 'natural' values, as symbolised by Caliban and Ariel – and, to Miranda's innocent eyes, by some of the arrivals from another shipwreck – inherently superior to those of the so-called civilised world? There is very little plot in *The Tempest*, less than in any of Shakespeare's previous thirty-five plays, and much ornate poetry, steeped in the metaphysical cadences of his great religious contemporaries. For what he clearly intends to be his swansong, in other words, unusually adopting the Aristotelian unities of time and place, Shakespeare embarks on nothing less than a philosophical discussion of the values which constitute civilisation. There could be no more majestic or appropriate coda. When writing Prospero's farewell to arms, Shakespeare was consciously writing his own.

The Tempest was first performed before the King in the Banqueting House at Whitehall on Hallowmas Night, 1 November, 1611. Shakespeare would have ridden down from Stratford for the occasion, enjoying an overnight stay en route in Oxford with the Davenants, dandling his five-year-old godson William on his knee. For by then he had retired to his rural roots.

By his forty-seventh birthday Shakespeare had returned home to Stratford, where he kept his own earthen half-pint mug at a local inn, 'out of which he was accustomed to take his draught of ale at a certain publick house every Saturday afternoon.' Anne was now fifty-four years old, their daughters in their mid-twenties. Susanna lived just around the corner from New Place, with her busy doctor husband and infant daughter; Judith was still at home with her parents, apparently unable to land as upstanding a husband, for she was now

(PAGES 282–283)
A MAP OF THE AMERICAN COASTLINE FROM VIRGINIA TO FLORIDA, DEPICTING THE VARIOUS SEA CREATURES INHABITING THE ATLANTIC OCEAN. FROM JOHN WHITE'S 'MAP OF THE ATLANTIC COAST', 1587.

almost as old as her 'on the shelf' mother when so carelessly impregnated by her father — who would now have to learn to be a family man for the first time in nearly thirty years of marriage.

It was not a role in which he had ever been well cast. At first he busied himself with property and financial transactions, even allowed himself to be tempted into town business like his father before him. In 1611 Mr Wm Shackspere is named by his kinsman and former lodger, the town clerk Thomas Greene, among subscribers cajoled into forking out 'towards the charge of prosecuting the bill in Parliament for the better repair of the highways and amending divers defects in the statutes already made'. And there were, as always, debts to collect; on 5 October 1611, just as he would have been heading south for rehearsals of *The Tempest*, a vintner and Henley Street neighbour named Robert Johnson, landlord of the White Lion, died owing £20 for 'a lease of a barn that he holdeth of Mr. Shaxper'.

On 3 February 1612 Shakespeare buried his brother Gilbert — dead, having never married, at the age of forty-five. Exactly a year later, on 4 February 1613, his brother Richard followed, also unmarried, at the age of thirty-eight. As he entered his fiftieth year, the oldest of the Shakespeare brothers was now the only one left living, the only one to have taken a wife and bred children. Of all of eight Shakespeare siblings, only William and his sister Joan, five years his junior (who would outlive him by thirty) now survived. For all his parents' longevity, Shakespeare's own generation was not faring well; after his own recent illness, it would hardly be surprising if, now more than ever, he felt a sense of living on borrowed time.

The portrait painted by most biographers, of a fulfilled Prospero now content to sit in his orchard counting his money, does not ring true. It did not take much for this supposedly 'retired' Shakespeare to be tempted back into writing for the King's Men. James's daughter, Elizabeth, was to be married on St Valentine's Day 1613 to Frederick, the Elector Palatine of the Rhine, a symbolic figure to European Protestants as claimant to the throne of Bohemia. A mere sixteen years old, like her husband-to-be, Elizabeth was the King's only surviving daughter. Major celebrations were planned — including, of course, a new play.

Since he had left the London field clear for his rivals, Shakespeare must have watched with mixed feelings as Ben Jonson advanced towards top billing, with such lesser lights as Webster, Chapman, Tourneur and Heywood all vying with him for the mantle of Marlowe. Could he really rest content that all these considerable talents merely confirmed his own effortless pre-eminence? The genteel life of Stratford was already beginning to bug him, as the town's growing Puritan element chose to snub its most famous son by banning all dramatic performances in the borough. If anything was calculated to drive Shakespeare back to London amid a hail of curses, fleeing the embrace of his weeping wife and daughters, that would do it.

As if to remind his rivals he was still around, he anyway had other reasons to remain a familiar figure on the London scene. In 1612 he rode south to give his evidence in that protracted litigation between his former landlords, the Mountjoys, and their son-in-law Stephen Belott. That same year also saw him complain to the printer William Jaggard about his new edition of *The Passionate Pilgrim*, first published in 1599 – but still containing five of Shakespeare's sonnets, still with his name on the title-page, and still without his knowledge or consent. Heywood, whose *Troia Britannica*, was similarly pirated for the same volume, seems to be trying to curry favour with Shakespeare by associating him with his own stern protest in an epistle to the printer appended to his *An Apology for Actors*. A chastened Jaggard promptly reprinted the title-page, omitting Shakespeare's name.

For all the detail of his love-hate relationship with Jonson, there is no record at all of Shakespeare's dealings with the other poet-playwrights of his day. But he evidently looked benignly on the work of Francis Beaumont and John Fletcher – twenty and fifteen years, respectively, his juniors – whose greater success as collaborators than as individuals perhaps posed no threat. Who asked whom we will never know – perhaps the King himself – but in 1612 Shakespeare saw fit to collaborate with Fletcher on at least one play, possibly two. The possible one is *Cardenio*, a lost work acted by the King's Men some time before 20 May 1613, and ascribed to

FRANCIS BEAUMONT, 1729.
ENGRAVING BY GEORGE VERTUE.

(OPPOSITE)
ELIZABETH, QUEEN OF
BOHEMIA, C.1610.
PAINTING BY
ROBERT PEAKE THE
ELDER, D.1619.

Shakespeare and Fletcher forty years later. The sure one is *Henry VIII*; the royal bride's name, after all, was Elizabeth.

Shakespeare's final plays for the King's Men had all been written with the Blackfriars in mind; they were playable at the Globe, but lacked the swaggering alfresco action which had proved such good box-office for so long. Burbage must have pleaded with his lifelong comrade-in-arms to think of their mutually beloved Globe, this time, as much as of Whitehall and the King. Either he felt he had to tread carefully, however, or the tired old playwright's heart wasn't really in it. *Le vrai* Shakespeare would have steeped himself in the unparalleled dramatic potential of Henry VIII's reign, from the neo-Falstaffian Bluff King Hal's cavalier treatment of all those wives to its grave religious consequences for Romanist families like the Shakespeares themselves. What emerged instead was a pallid, pompous, prettified version of events from 1520 to 1533, from the Field of the Cloth of Gold to the christening of Princess Elizabeth.

The play's empty emphasis on pomp and pageantry — one of the few theatrical reasons why it still enjoys occasional revivals — confirms that *Henry VIII* was one of no fewer than fourteen plays, six of them by Shakespeare, performed between the royal wedding on 14 February 1613 and the happy couple's departure for Germany two months later. To see his players revive *Much Ado About Nothing*, *Othello*, *The Winter's Tale* and *The Tempest* would have reminded the melancholy King of happier times. James's heir, Henry, had died the previous November, aged only eighteen; now his younger brother, Charles, was finding it hard to fulfil Henry's promise. Hence, perhaps, James's determination to marry off his favourite daughter in such extravagant style, lavishing no less than £6,000 on a mock sea battle on the Thames. The King's Men, by contrast, received a mere £93 6s 8d for their pains, on top of £50 for six other court performances that season.

Four months after its royal première, on the afternoon of 29 June 1613, a performance of *Henry VIII* at the Globe ended abruptly soon after Act I, Scene 4, line 49 — 'Look out there, some of ye' — when a spark from the firing of a cannon to mark the King's arrival at Cardinal Wolsey's house strayed into the theatre's thatched roof, starting a fire which saw the building razed to the

(OPPOSITE)
CLAUDIO AND ISABELLA,
FROM 'MEASURE FOR
MEASURE'.
PAINTING BY WILLIAM
HOLMAN HUNT,
1827–1910.

ground within an hour. No-one was hurt — 'nothing did perish but wood and straw, and a few forsaken cloaks' — although one man's breeches caught fire, 'that would perhaps have broiled him, if he had not by the benefit of a provident wit put it out with a bottled ale'.

Puritans saw the hand of God in the 'sudden fearful burning' of the 'straw-thatched house' beside the Thames. To the players themselves, not to mention the shareholders — and, indeed, posterity — it was of course a catastrophe. Just as Prospero forecast, the great Globe itself had dissolved — and, with it, who knows what? How many manuscripts of Shakespeare's plays, accurate prompt copies of works we think we know, as well as others we never will? Not to mention costumes, properties and other worldlier goods representing months and years of work, the livelihoods of those with nothing to fall back on. 'See the world's ruins,' sympathised Ben Jonson.

And yet within a year, on 30 June 1614, one diary-keeping Londoner called on a friend, only to be told that she had 'gone to the Globe, to a play'. From the ashes of Shakespeare's original 'wooden O', like the phoenix in Cranmer's undelivered tribute to Elizabeth that terrible afternoon in 1613, arose 'another heir / As great in admiration as herself' — a new Globe, this one with a tiled roof. Who had paid for it? There were rumours that the King himself corraled his richer sycophants into coughing up, however reluctantly, to replace the noble building ravaged during that glutinous celebration of himself and his predecessor, even though neither of them (whatever Tom Stoppard would have us believe of Queen Elizabeth in the film *Shakespeare in Love*) had ever actually set foot in the place.

More likely, the costs would have been borne by the shareholders, required by the terms of their lease to underwrite the maintenance of the building. By one account, 'each sharer was at first assessed £50 or £60 towards the charges, but ended up having to pay much more'. At least one went broke in the process. Shakespeare, with one foot in Stratford and an eye ever to the main chance, might well have seen this as the moment to cut his losses, sell off his stake in the business, and make a second attempt to spend more time with his family in rural retirement in Stratford, leaving London and the theatre behind him.

(OPPOSITE)
HENRY VIII, C.1536.
PAINTING BY UNKNOWN
ARTIST AFTER HANS
HOLBEIN.

So did the forty-nine-year-old poet, as has been seductively suggested, brood over the razing of the Globe 'while pruning the Great Garden of New Place', and decide that this was 'a good time to sell his seventh share of the moiety in the company which he had served, to the best of his abilities, for nigh on two decades'?

No, he assuredly did not. He may have seized the moment to cash in his chips at the Globe, but not to ease his (already comfortably-off) retirement in the bosom of the family with whom he was always so ill at ease. Since earlier that year, while in London for the wedding of the King's daughter, and at least three months before the fire at the Globe, Shakespeare had been negotiating to buy the gate-house of the former Blackfriars monastery beside the Thames — little more than a hundred yards from the stage-door of the Blackfriars Theatre.

Originally part of the huge Dominican priory at Blackfriars, the gate-house was described as a 'dwelling-house or tenement' built over a 'great gate' at the head of a street leading down to the river at Puddle Wharf, where wherries waited to taxi customers across the river to Bankside and the Globe. Shakespeare paid £140, including £80 up front in cash. His closest friend Richard Burbage lived nearby; close to their favourite tavern, let alone both theatres in which the King's Men plied their trade, the gate-house was the perfect London *pied-à-terre* for Shakespeare. For the next year at least, until failing health finally drove him back to his family for good, the Blackfriars gate-house was Shakespeare's home-from-home. His brief, half-hearted attempt at retirement to Stratford had made him realise how bored he would be in his native rural backwater, for all his fondness (tinged with guilt) for his daughters. London, for all its petty irritations, had long since replaced Warwickshire as his natural habitat.

An entry in the Stationers Register for 8 April 1634 and the title-page of a subsequent quarto edition assure us that *The Two Noble Kinsmen* was a 'Tragi-Comedy' by 'the memorable Worthies of their time, Mr John Fletcher, and Mr William Shakespeare, Gent[lemen]', which had oft been presented at the Blackfriars 'by the King's Majesty's servants with great applause'. We also know from a 'scrap of paper' emanating from the King's Office of the Revels that *The*

(PAGES 292–293)
THE FIELD OF THE
CLOTH OF GOLD.
UNKNOWN ARTIST.
(OPPOSITE)
POSTHUMUS AND IMOGEN
IN 'CYMBELINE', FROM
'CHILDREN'S STORIES
FROM SHAKESPEARE' BY
EDITH NESBIT, 1858–1924.

Two Noble Kinsmen was in the repertory of the King's Men by 1619, probably long before, but was only now being 'considered for performance at court'. A great success, by all accounts, in the few years left to Shakespeare, and over the next few decades, *The Two Noble Kinsmen* has since fared less well. Revived by the ferociously loyal William Davenant in 1664, in a typically free adaptation entitled *The Rivals,* the play was rarely performed over the two centuries and more before it was boldly chosen to open the Royal Shakespeare Company's new Elizabethan-style auditorium in Stratford, The Swan, in 1986.

By his fiftieth birthday, in April 1614, Shakespeare finally was back in Stratford, his health gradually beginning to fail, his family rallying round. Now he found himself doubly fortunate in his son-in-law, John Hall, not only a good and loving husband to Susanna, but a sound and dutiful physician to his father-in-law.

Shakespeare's glory days in the capital might finally be over – now, his private grief no doubt mitigated by the extra income, he could rent out the Blackfriars gate-house – but he was still as determined as ever to enjoy himself. His lifelong friend, coeval and fellow Warwickshire poet-playwright, Michael Drayton, who had collaborated on dramas with Dekker, Webster, even Henry Chettle, but never with Shakespeare, often stayed with highly civilised mutual friends, Sir Henry and Lady (Anne) Rainsford, barely two miles across the Avon in the village of Clifford Chambers. Drayton would bring the latest gossip from London, as ready to trash rising reputations as he was to reminisce. Ben Jonson, with whom uncomplicated friendship appears to have blossomed from years of rivalry, was eager to stay in touch, even pay the occasional visit to Stratford as he walked the length and breadth of the nation, in a vain attempt to lose weight. Shakespeare was godfather to one of Jonson's children; 'I'll e'en give him a dozen latten spoons,' he had written to Ben, 'and thou shalt translate them'. So Jonson, it seems, was already teasing Shakespeare about his 'small' Latin.

Perhaps retirement would not be so dull and dispiriting, after all. For another thing, Shakespeare could gratify his father's ghost by lording it over the locals, entertaining at New Place such notable visitors as the visiting

(OPPOSITE)
HENRY, PRINCE OF
WALES.
PAINTING BY
ISAAC OLIVER.

preacher invited to give the Whitsuntide sermon; the borough corporation even subsidised him to the tune of 20d for 'one quart of sack and one quart of claret wine' to keep his house-guest happy. That summer, on 9 July, New Place and his other properties were fortunate to escape a 'sudden and terrible fire' which swept through Stratford, the third in living memory. Boosted by a high wind, its force was 'so great … that it dispersed into so many places thereof whereby the whole town was in very great danger to have been utterly consumed.' More than fifty dwelling-houses were razed, along with stables and barns storing precious grain and hay.

UNATTRIBUTED ENGRAVING FROM 'THE WOEFULL AND LAMENTABLE WAST AND SPOILE DONE BY A SUDDAINE FIRE IN ST EDMONDS-BURY', 1610.

There was a collection for the victims, to which we can only assume that Shakespeare contributed. But the patron saint of fellow-feeling was not averse to standing on his dignity when his own financial interests were at stake. That same summer of 1614 saw the start of a tumultuous local dispute which would not be finally resolved until after his death. It affected men of property, and it affected men of none – those who supported their families by working on the soil. The dispute over 'enclosure', in short, affected everyone, high and low, in ways which might be expected to have earned Shakespeare's sympathy. But he maintained a judicious public silence throughout, watchful for his own interests.

If Susanna's husband, John Hall, was proving himself the very model of a Jacobean gentleman, Judith's husband-to-be would prove quite the opposite. Dr Hall, who had come to Stratford via Cambridge in 1600, was one of the most dedicated and sought-after physicians in the region, working tirelessly day and night to apply his patent remedies to the ailments of both rich and poor, aristocrats and their servants. So respected did Hall become that the corporation tried to draft him in as an unelected burgess; so professionally popular was he that he felt obliged to decline their generous offer because of pressure of work. His eloquent case-books are full of innovative herbal reme-

(OPPOSITE)
SIX MINIATURE PORTRAITS
OF THE FAMILY TREE OF
KING JAMES I.
BY NICHOLAS HILLIARD
AND ISAAC OLIVER.

dies for all afflictions, major and minor, crammed with fascinating period detail on treatments for conditions from dropsy to scurvy, the itch to the pox, not hesitating to detail those applied to the ailments of all his patients, down to his own wife and daughter, even himself. Hall's Puritan views and stern record as a churchwarden may make the worthy doctor seem something of a prig. But he proved otherwise by standing by his wife in her potentially ruinous hour of most need, when she was falsely accused of infidelity with one Rafe Smith.

Susanna's sister Judith was less fortunate in her own eventual choice of a husband, Thomas Quiney, son of Shakespeare's importunate friend Richard, who had written that begging letter all of eighteen years before. A vintner by trade, young Quiney was twenty-six, and Judith thirty-one, when they married at Holy Trinity on 10 February 1616. Any uncomfortable memories that may have spoilt the day for the bride's mother, herself eight years older than her husband, were staunched by the drama surrounding the event. Shortly before their wedding day, Judith had discovered that another local woman, Margaret Wheeler, was pregnant by her husband-to-be. Hence, perhaps, their own o'er-hasty progress to the altar. Within a month of their nuptials, Margaret Wheeler died in childbirth, and her infant with her. Both were buried, according to the parish register, on 15 March.

Quiney's was a crime far worse than the harmless fornication-before-marriage which had seen Claudio condemned to death in his father-in-law's sombre *Measure for Measure*. On 26 March, eleven days after his wedding, Judith's husband was summoned before the local vicar's ecclesiastical court, where he pleaded guilty to 'carnal copulation' and was sentenced to perform public penance by wearing a white sheet in church on three successive Sundays. Whether or not the influential Shakespeare intervened, to spare his daughter this dire humiliation as much as her husband, we have no way of knowing. But Quiney's sentence was mysteriously commuted, within days, to a meagre fine of five shillings, and a private display of penitence to another local vicar rather than an extended public ordeal. The newlyweds' blushes were spared; but their marriage was not, to say the least, off to the best of starts.

Quiney subsequently lived up to these dubious beginnings, thwarting his

(PAGES 300–301)
MIRANDA, FROM 'THE TEMPEST'.
PAINTING BY JOHN WILLIAM WATERHOUSE, 1849–1917.

own attempts to achieve local respectability on the town council with a long track-record of drunken scrapes. He allowed his chums to drink illegally in his house; watered down the wine at his inn, the Cage; and eventually tried to cheat his wife by selling the family business behind her back. Shakespeare's surviving kinsmen, long after his death, intervened in time to protect his daughter's interests. But Judith had married a bad lot, and can be excused for suspecting some sort of divine retribution when all three of her children by Quiney died long before her. The first, christened Shakespeare Quiney a year after his grandfather's death, perished in infancy on 8 May 1617. Two more sons, Richard and Thomas, born over the following three years, both died within a month of each other in 1639, aged twenty-one and nineteen.

Susanna was literate, Judith was not. Shakespeare may have taken more pride in his more refined, worldly-wise, locally respected older daughter, but he knew that he had not been much of a father to either. His ghost would probably shrug with fatalistic resignation at the failure of both to keep his name alive. Susanna never had more than the one daughter, Elizabeth, who herself died childless (despite two marriages) in 1670, at the age of sixty-one. Nor did Judith ever have any more children; she died in 1662, at the remarkable age of seventy-seven, having outlived her older sister by thirteen years. Within a generation, the Shakespeare line was extinct. Never expecting his writings to outlive him, and knowing that his brothers had all failed to preserve the family name, John Shakespeare's son appeared to have wasted his time securing that proud family crest and motto.

It was surely at Judith's wedding reception that Shakespeare enjoyed the 'merry meeting' with his old friends Jonson and Drayton at which they 'drank too much', giving the Stratford man the fever from which he would never recover. Judith's twin brother, his son Hamnet, dead these twenty years, would obviously have been on his mind that day; further depressed by the dubious marriage his daughter was making, and the dire developments overshadowing the ceremony, perhaps this man of moderation in most things did for once permit himself to over-indulge.

Shakespeare had never been much of 'a company keeper', as Aubrey heard it from his friend (and fellow actor) Christopher Beeston's son, William. He 'wouldn't be debauched' – to the point of telling white lies; 'if invited', he would pretend that he was 'in pain.' On this occasion, however, he himself was the host; and his two fellow writers would surely have brightened up the dreary guest-list of Stratford worthies at his second daughter's wedding, typified by the local physician and cleric, John Ward, whose memoir is the only witness we have of the events leading up to Shakespeare's death:

> *Shakespeare, Drayton and Ben Jonson, had a merry meeting, and it seems*
> *drank too much, for Shakespeare died of a fever there contracted.*

William Shakespeare died on 23 April 1616, supposedly his fifty-second birthday.

Six months earlier, he had revised his will to prevent Quiney getting his hands on Judith's money. As Susanna became the chatelaine of New Place, however, Shakespeare's will is more celebrated for his apparently insulting bequest of his 'second-best bed' to his wife, the former Anne Hathaway. But Elizabethan and Jacobean custom and practice in fact suggests that the Shakespeares, like most well-to-do middle-class couples, would have reserved the best bed in their home for overnight guests. Now, in turn, this would have passed to their older daughter. The 'second-best' bed Shakespeare so famously specified in his will was, therefore, the marital bed he had shared with Anne – on and off, to put it mildly – for more than thirty years (and perhaps her own parents' bed before that). Far from signifying the rottenness of their marriage, the bequest suggests a touching vote of thanks from a grateful husband, aware of his own shortcomings, for the long-suffering, dogged loyalty of a partner who had for years put up with a long-distance marriage, single-handedly brought up his children in his absence, and overlooked his own all too evident lapses when he did choose to put in the occasional appearance at home.

For all his strenuous attempts to keep within the family the huge legacy purchased by his genius, Shakespeare's wordly goods would soon be disbursed amid a wide array of less than close relations, who, whether or not they perused his writings, would bless his memory for generations to come. We who come later must bless the memory of John Heminges and Henry Condell, the King's Men who spent the next seven years gathering together the scattered texts of their friend and fellow-actor's plays, and checking and re-checking their embattled texts before publishing them in what we call the First Folio. The volume entitled *Mr William Shakespeare's Comedies, Histories and Tragedies* was entered in the Stationers Register on 8 November 1623, and published by Edward Blount and Isaac Jaggard soon after. With a Shakespearean eye to the main chance, Heminges and Condell dedicated the book to potential future patrons, the theatre-loving William Herbert, third Earl of Pembroke, and his younger brother Philip, first Earl of Montgomery. Twelve years since the publication of the Authorised Version of the Holy Bible which he had himself commissioned, the reign of King James I had now seen the publication, barely a decade apart, of the two most important books in the English language.

Shakespeare had no reason to expect his plays to outlive him, let alone hold the stage the world over four centuries after his death. There was no precedent for the publication of a collection of dramatic works. Later in the year of his death, 1616, Ben Jonson would become the first to enjoy such an accolade in his own lifetime; seven years later, he was minded to pay handsome tribute to his great contemporary in a preface to his collected works, in the shape of the verses addressed 'To the memory of my beloved, the author Mr William Shakespeare, and what he hath left us'.

Soul of the Age!

The applause! delight! the wonder of our stage!

My Shakespeare, rise! . . .

He was not of an age, but for all time!

It is, at the last, for the reader to decide whether this serves as a better epitaph than the curmudgeonly one Shakespeare wrote for himself, apparently trying to frighten posterity into letting him rest in peace, leaving his plays and poems to speak for him:

(PAGES 306–307)
THE PRINCE'S CHOICE.
THOMAS REYNOLDS
LAMONT, 1826–98.

GOOD FREND FOR JESUS SAKE FORBEARE,

TO DIGG THE DUST ENCLOSED HEARE:

BLESTE BE YE MAN THAT SPARES THESE STONES,

AND CURST BE HE THAT MOVES MY BONES.

Mr. WILLIAM
SHAKESPEARES
COMEDIES,
HISTORIES, &
TRAGEDIES.

Published according to the True Originall Copies.

Martin Droeshout sculpsit London.

LONDON
Printed by Isaac Iaggard, and Ed. Blount. 1623.

Chronology of Shakespeare's work

1595–96

King John

1587–92

1 Henry VI

2 Henry VI

3 Henry VI

Richard III

The Two Gentlemen of Verona

Titus Andronicus

[*contrib*. Edward III]

1592

Venus and Adonis

1593–94

The Rape of Lucrece

1593–1600

Sonnets [*published* 1609]

1593–94

The Comedy of Errors

The Taming of the Shrew

Love's Labour's Lost

1594–95

Midsummer Night's Dream

Romeo and Juliet

The Merchant of Venice

1595

Richard II

1596–97

1 Henry IV

1597

The Merry Wives of Windsor

1598

2 Henry IV

1598–99

Much Ado About Nothing

1599

Henry V

Julius Caesar

As You Like It

1600–1

Hamlet

1601

'The Phoenix and Turtle'

1601–2

Troilus and Cressida

Twelfth Night

1602–3

All's Well That Ends Well

1603

[*contrib*. Sir Thomas More]

1604

Measure for Measure

Othello

1605

King Lear

1606

Macbeth

1606–7

Antony and Cleopatra

1607–8

Timon of Athens

Coriolanus

1607–8

Pericles

1609–10

Cymbeline

1610–11

The Winter's Tale

1611

The Tempest

1612–13

Henry VIII [*with* Fletcher]

1613

The Two Noble Kinsmen [*with* Fletcher]

Shakespeare's Family Tree

RICHARD SHAKESPEARE
OF SNITTERFIELD
D. 1561

ROBERT ARDEN
OF ASBIES, WILMCOTE
D. DEC. 1556

JOHN SHAKESPEARE
D. SEPT. 1601
=
MARY ARDEN
D. SEPT. 1608

JOAN
B. SEPT. 1558
D. IN INFANCY

MARGARET
B. NOV. 1562
D. IN INFANCY

WILLIAM
B. APRIL 1564
D. APRIL 1616
=
ANNE
(NEÉ HATHAWAY)
B. 1556 D. 1623

GILBERT
B. OCT. 1566
D. FEB. 1612

JOAN
B. APRIL 1569
D. NOV. 1646
=
WILLIAM HART
HATTER OF STRATFORD
D. APRIL 1616

ANNE
B. SEPT. 1571
D. APRIL 1579

RICHARD
B. MAR. 1574
D. FEB. 1613

EDMUND
B. MAY 1580
D. DEC. 1607

SUSANNA
B. MAY 1583
D. JULY 1649
=
JOHN HALL
B. 1575
D. NOV. 1635

HAMNET
B. JAN. 1585
D. AUG. 1596

JUDITH
B. JAN. 1585
D. JAN. 1662
=
THOMAS QUINEY
VINTNER OF STRATFORD
B. 1589 D. 1655

WILLIAM
B. AUG. 1600
D. MAR. 1639

MARY
B. JUNE 1603
D. DEC. 1607

THOMAS
B. JULY 1605
D. 1670

MICHAEL
B. SEPT. 1608
D. NOV. 1618

ELIZABETH
B. DEC. 1607
D. FEB. 1670
=
THOMAS NASH
B. 1593
D. APRIL 1647

SHAKESPEARE
B. NOV. 1616
D. MAY 1617

RICHARD
B. FEB. 1617
D. JAN. 1639
(NO ISSUE)

THOMAS
B. JAN. 1619
D. JAN. 1639

THOMAS
B. APRIL 1634

GEORGE
B. SEPT. 1636
D. 1702

=
JOHN, LATER SIR JOHN
BARNARD OF ABINGTON
D. 1674 (NO ISSUE)

JOAN

SUSANNA

SHAKESPEARE

(LINE OF HARTS CONTINUED)

311

Source Notes

PROLOGUE

'not because we do not know enough':
Harold Bloom, *The Western Canon* (New York:
Harcourt Brace, 1994), p. 61.

'the right of every Shakespeare-lover': Anthony
Burgess, *Shakespeare* (London: Vintage, 1996), p. 9.

'the finer weapon, the sharper point': Henry
James, introduction to *The Tempest* in Sidney
Lee (ed.), *The Complete Works of William
Shakespeare*, Vol. XVI (London: John Murray,
1906–9), reprinted in Henry James, *Essays on
Literature: American and English Writers* (New York:
New American Library, 1984), pp. 1219–20.

'the apparently boundless hospitality of his
imagination': John Jones, *Shakespeare at Work*
(Oxford: Clarendon Press, 1995), p. 12.

'We ask and ask': John Bryson (ed.), *Matthew
Arnold, Poetry and Prose* (London: Hart-Davis,
1954), p. 32.

'We do not understand Shakespeare from a
single reading': T. S. Eliot, 'Dante' (1929), *Selected
Essays* (London: Faber & Faber, 1932), p. 245.

'We cannot know, by reading Shakespeare' …
'he did not like lawyers': Harold Bloom,
Shakespeare: The Invention of the Human
(New York: Riverhead, 1998), pp. 7–8.

'If you read and re-read Shakespeare endlessly':
Harold Bloom, *The Western Canon*, p. 53.

'We read, those of us who do': John Updike,
New York Review of Books, Vol. XLVI, No. 2,
4 February 1999.

'everyone … borrows from earlier writers':
E. A. J. Honigmann, *Shakespeare: The Lost Years*
(Manchester: MUP, 1985, revised 1998), p. vii.

I
STRATFORD: 1564–1569

'in honour of her famous relation':
De Quincey in Samuel Schoenbaum,
William Shakespeare: A Compact Documentary Life
(Oxford: OUP, 1987), p. 25.

'able-bodied citizens': Schoenbaum, op. cit., p. 33.

'very honest, sober, industrious': Schoenbaum,
op. cit., p. 33.

'Three or four thousand or more of the
Testaments': J. de Groot, *The Shakespeares and
'The Old Faith'* (1946), p. 88.

'clear their houses of all show of suspicion':
Peter Milward, *Shakespeare's Religious Background*
(London: Sidgwick & Jackson, 1973), p. 21.

II
CHILDHOOD: 1569–1579

'small Latin and less Greek': Ben Jonson,
commendatory verses prefacing the First
Folio of Shakespeare's *Collected Works*, 1623.

'pronouncing of letters, syllables, and words':
Schoenbaum, op. cit., p. 64.

'To learne to wrytte doune Ingglisshe':
Burgess, op. cit., p. 29.

'as well qualified in Latin': Stanley Wells,
Shakespeare: A Dramatic Life (London:
Sinclair-Stevenson, 1994), p. 13.

'Quotations from … forty-two books of the
Bible': Richmond Noble, *Shakespeare's Biblical
Knowledge and Use of the Book of Common Prayer,
as Exemplified in the Plays of the First Folio*
(London: SPCK, 1935), p. 20.

'in the office of some county attorney':
Edmund Malone, 'An Attempt to Ascertain
the Order in Which the Plays Attributed to
Shakespeare Were Written', in Shakespeare,
Plays and Poems, ed. Edmund Malone
(London: J. Rivington & Sons, 1790), Vol. I,
Part I, p. 307.

'to the extreme end of ruin': 'William
Shakespeare', entry in *Biographica Britannica*
(1747–66), Vol. VI, Part I, p. 3628, quoted in
E. K. Chambers, *William Shakespeare: A Study of
Facts and Problems* (Oxford: Clarendon Press,
1930), p. 287.

'excepting the three dates 1582, 1583 and 1585':
Honigmann, op. cit., p. 1.

'normally went to university': T. W. Baldwin, *Shakespeare's 'Small Latine and Lesse Greeke'*, (1944), Vol. 1, p. 487.

III
The 'Lost' Years: 1579–1587

No scholar has done more than E. A. J. Honigmann (*Shakespeare: The Lost Years*) to put flesh on the bones of an idea 'first suggested', as he concedes, by Oliver Baker's *In Shakespeare's Warwickshire and the Unknown Years* (London: Simpkin Marshall, 1937), 're-stated' by E. K. Chambers in 'William Shakeshafte', *Shakespearean Gleanings* (London: OUP, 1944), taken further by Alan Keen and Roger Lubbock in *The Annotator* (London: Putnam, 1954). Honigmann is endorsed cautiously by S. Schoenbaum (*Times Literary Supplement*, 19 April 1985, and in the 1987 edition of *A Compact Documentary Life*) and enthusiastically by Eric Sams (*The Real Shakespeare*). The argument was further advanced by Richard Wilson in 'Shakespeare and the Jesuits', *Times Literary Supplement*, 19 December 1997, and at 'Lancastrian Shakespeare', a conference held in part at Hoghton Tower under the auspices of Lancaster University's Shakespeare Programme, 21–24 July 1999.

'a schoolmaster in the country': Oliver Lawson Dick (ed.), *Aubrey's Brief Lives* (Harmondsworth: Penguin, 1962), p. 276.

'one of the premier families of Lancashire': Honigmann, op. cit., p. 8.

'to retain the Queen's Majesty's subjects in due obedience': J. Stanley Leatherbarrow, *The Lancashire Elizabethan Recusants* (Manchester, 1947), p. 55.

'especially the house of Richard Hoghton': *Acts of the Privy Council*, Vol. XIII, p. 149, quoted in Honigmann, op. cit., p. 10.

'Being taken from school': Sir Thomas Elyot, *The Boke Named the Governour* (London, 1531), quoted in Joseph Quincy Adams, *A Life of William Shakespeare* (London: Constable, 1923), pp. 61–2.

'Baker' for 'Barbar': J. W. Gray, 'Hathway or Whateley', *Shakespeare's Marriage* (London: Chapman & Hall, 1905), pp. 21–35.

IV
London: 1587–1592

'an indifferent actor': Shakespearean actors are fond of disputing this. 'You didn't get billing as a tragedian with the King's Men unless you could act,' insists one such, Peter O'Toole, who believes that Shakespeare was 'one of life's Mercutios'. (Author's conversation with O'Toole, 20 June 1999; Anthony Holden, 'Men Behaving Bardly', *Observer*, 11 July 1999.)

'Behold these sumptuous houses' … 'an evident token of a wicked time': T[homas] W[hite], 'A Sermon preached at Pawles Cross on Sunday the thirde of November 1577 in the time of the Plague' (London, 1578), p. 47, quoted in Chambers, *Elizabethan Stage*, p. 269; William Harrison, MS 'Chronologie', quoted in ibid.

'a butcher's apprentice would be useful': Sams, op. cit., p. 55.

'poor' … 'without money and friends': Ibid., p. 56.

'receiv'd into the Company': Nicholas Rowe, op. cit., p. vi.

'first office in the theatre': Edmond Malone, *Supplement to the Edition of Shakespeare's Plays Published in 1778 by S. Johnson and G. Steevens* (London: Bathurst, 1780), p. 67.

'one of the first actors in Shakespeare's plays': Seymour Pitcher, *The Case for Shakespeare's Authorship of 'The Famous Victories of Henry V'* (London: Alvin Redman, 1961), p. 175.

'The handwriting of his signature on the book suggests as much': Sir Edward Thompson, *Shakespeare's Handwriting: A Study* (Oxford: Clarendon Press, 1916); 'Special Transcript of the Three Pages', *Shakespeare's Hand in the Play of Sir Thomas More*, ed. A. W. Pollard (Cambridge: CUP, 1923), quoted in Sams, op. cit., p. 72.

'How it would have joyed brave Talbot': Thomas Nashe, *Pierce Penniless* (London, 1592).

'horror turns to pity': Herschel Baker, Introduction to *1–3 Henry VI* in *The Riverside Shakespeare* (Boston, MA: Houghton Mifflin, 1974), p. 592.

'Edward III': See Eric Sams, *Shakespeare's Edward III* (New Haven, CT: Yale University Press, 1996).

'The cause of plague is sin': F. P. Wilson, *The Plague in Shakespeare's London* (Oxford: Clarendon Press, 1927), p. 52.

V
THE 'UPSTART CROW': 1592–1594

'Whoever she was, she enchanted the poet': Jonathan Bate, *Mail on Sunday*, 14 February 1999.

'You must believe in Mrs Florio': Jonathan Bate, *The Genius of Shakespeare* (London: Picador, 1997), p. 58.

'definitive … unanswerable': A. L. Rowse, *Shakespeare's Sonnets* (London: Macmillan, 1964, third edition 1984), pp. xix-xxv.

'a well known person … of superior social standing': Ibid.

'anonymous, even composite': Burgess, op. cit., p. 131.

'happy endings must, to carry conviction': Barton, Introduction to the Riverside edition of *The Comedy of Errors*, p. 81.

'an unconscious desire': A. Bronson Feldman, *International Journal of Psycho-Analysis*, Vol. XXXVI, 1955, quoted in the Arden edition of *The Comedy of Errors*, op. cit., n. 1.

VI
THE LORD CHAMBERLAIN'S MAN: 1594–1599

'disordered tumult and crowd': See *Gesta Grayorum: or, The History of the High and Mighty Prince Henry, Prince of Purpoole …* (London: W. Canning, 1688).

'the most complete man of the theater of his time': G. E. Bentley, *Shakespeare: A Biographical Handbook* (New Haven, CT: Yale University Press, 1961), p. 119.

'Few in any age have served the stage so variously': Schoenbaum, op. cit., p. 185.

'play of the hour': Sir Sidney Lee, *The Gentleman's Magazine*, February 1880, pp. 185–200, quoted in the Arden edition of *Romeo and Juliet*, ed. John Russell Brown (London: Methuen, 1964), p. xxiii.

'mythical beasts: strange, evil beings': Barton, Introduction to the Riverside edition of *The Merchant of Venice*, p. 250.

'a vice most odious': D. L. Thomas and N. E. Evans, 'John Shakespeare in the Exchequer', *Shakespeare Quarterly*, Vol. XXXV, 1984, pp. 315–18.

'humanity and good nature': Rowe, op. cit., pp. xii-xiii.

'looked on approvingly': Schoenbaum, op. cit., p. 207.

VII
THE GLOBE: 1599–1603

'went with my party across the water': Ernest Schanzer, 'Thomas Platter's Observations on the Elizabethan Stage', *Notes and Queries* (1956), p. 466.

'habits of business': J. O. Halliwell-Phillips, 'A Life of William Shakespeare', in Shakespeare, *Works* (1853–65), p. 151.

'so old and out of use': Francis Bacon, *Declaration of the Practises and Treasons* (London, 1601), quoted in Schoenbaum, op. cit, p. 218.

'I am Richard II': Chambers, op. cit., pp. 326–7.

VIII
THE KING'S MAN: 1603–1606

'played at court no fewer than 187 times': G. E. Bentley, 'Shakespeare and the Blackfriars Theatre', *Shakespeare Survey I* (Cambridge: CUP, 1948), p. 40.

'We have the man Shakespeare with us': *Extracts from the Letters and Journals of William Cory*, ed. Francis Warre Cornish (London, 1897), p. 168, quoted in Chambers, op. cit., p. 329, reports that in 1865 the Countess of Pembroke's descendant, Lady Herbert, told a visiting Eton master named William Cory that the family still possessed this letter; but it has never come to light.

'her teeth were made in Blackfriars': Ben Jonson, *Epicoene*, quoted in Schoenbaum, op. cit., pp. 260–1.

'a man among men': Wallace, ibid.

'Mary Mountjoy alained': Rowse, 'Secrets of Shakespeare's Landlady', *The Times*, 23 April 1973.

'strange in their ways' . . . 'barbarians': Arden edition of *Othello*, ed. Honigmann (London: Methuen, 1997), p. 2.

'Choke the devil! Choke him!': A. C. Sprague, *Shakespeare and the Actors* (Cambridge, MA: Harvard University Press, 1945), p. 199.

'whether the imagination can produce real effects': Kermode, Introduction to the Riverside edition of *Macbeth*, p. 1308.

IX
BLACKFRIARS: 1606–1611

'whether for the beautiful mistress of the house': Charles Gildon (ed.), *The Lives and Characters of the English Dramatick Poets . . . by Gerard Langbaine* (London, 1698), p. 32.

'In all probability he got him': Bodleian Library MS, Hearne Diaries.

'pretty certain that I shall be hanged' . . . 'Milton saved him from execution': Hamilton, op. cit., p. 18.

'turn his back on London': Burgess, op. cit., p. 209.

'overgrown schoolboys with "crazed" notions of privilege': Wyndham Lewis, *The Lion and the Fox*, quoted in Frank Kermode, Introduction to the Riverside edition of *Coriolanus*, p. 1392.

'Joan for Joanna, Eleanor for Helen' . . . 'Someone of means': G. E. Bentley, *Shakespeare: A Biographical Handbook* (New Haven, CT: Yale University Press, 1961), p. 81.

'the depths of despair' . . . 'an elderly serenity': Edward Dowden, *Shakspere: His Mind and Art* (London, 1875), quoted in Kermode, Arden edition of *The Tempest* (London: Methuen, 1954), p. lxxxii.

'a serious illness' . . . 'a nervous breakdown': E. K. Chambers, *A Short Life of Shakespeare* (Oxford: Clarendon Press, 1933), p. 61.

'too intimate' . . . 'eternity promised by our ever-living poet': Schoenbaum, op. cit., p. 270.

'Much scholarship has been devoted': See Leslie Hotson, *Mr W.H.* (London: Chatto & Windus, 1964).

'literalists of the imagination': Lines subsequently excised from the original version of *Poetry*, Marianne Moore, *Collected Poems* (London: Faber & Faber, 1951), pp. 266–7.

'philosopher of roguery': Ibid., p. 1566.

X
'A MERRY MEETING': 1611–1616

'out of which he was accustomed to take his draught': George Steevens, note on Sir John Oldcastle, in Malone's *Supplement to the Edition of Shakespeare's Plays Published in 1778 by Samuel Johnson and George Steevens*, op. cit., pp. 369–70.

'nothing did perish but wood and straw' . . . 'that would perhaps have broiled him' . . . 'certain chambers being shot off': Sir Henry Wotton, letter to Sir Edmund Bacon, quoted in Logan Pearsall Smith, *The Life and Letters of Sir Henry Wotton* (Oxford: Clarendon Press, 1907), p. 17; see also Chambers, op. cit., p. 153.

'gone to the Globe, to a play' . . . 'rumours that the King himself' . . . 'each sharer was at first assessed £50 or £60' . . . 'while pruning' . . . 'this was a good time to sell': Schoenbaum, op. cit, p. 277.

'whatever Tom Stoppard would have us believe': In the penultimate scene of the Oscar-winning film *Shakespeare in Love* (Miramax, 1998, co-written by Sir Tom Stoppard), the Queen unexpectedly steps out from the audience at the Globe to sort out problems between Shakespeare, his beloved Lady Viola (Gwyneth Paltrow) and her equally fictitious husband.

'dwelling-house or tenement' . . . 'great gate' . . . 'all and singular cellars': Conveyance dated 10 March 1613, quoted in Schoenbaum, op. cit., p. 273.

'scrap of paper' . . . 'considered for performance at court': Hallett Smith, Introduction to the Riverside edition of *The Two Noble Kinsmen*, p. 1639.

Index

Picture Acknowledgements

AKG 5, 15, 25, 26, 42–43, 83, 109, 111, 139, 144, 153, 202, 238-9, 272-3, 308; The Art Archive 177, 184, 210–211; Ashmolean Museum 148; Agnew & Sons, London, UK/Bridgeman Art Library 2, National Gallery of Scotland, Edinburgh, Scotland/Bridgeman Art Library 6, Private Collection/The Stapleton Collection/Bridgeman Art Library 8, 11, 12, 14, Phillips, The International Fine Art Auctioneers, UK/Bridgeman Art Library 16, Private Collection/Christie's Images/Bridgeman Art Library 48, Roy Miles Fine Paintings/Bridgeman Art Library 66, New Walk Museum, Leicester City Museum Service, UK/Bridgeman Art Library 70–71, Oldham Art Gallery, Lancashire, UK/Bridgeman Art Library 76, Private Collection/Julian Hartnoll, London, UK/Bridgeman Art Library 79, Delaware Art Museum, Wilmington, DE, USA/Visual Arts Library, London, UK/Samuel and Mary R. Bancroft Memorial/Bridgeman Art Library 80, St Faith's Church, Gaywood, Norfolk, UK/Bridgeman Art Library 92–93, Philip Mould, Historical Portraits Ltd, London, UK/Bridgeman Art Library 112, Johannesburg Art Gallery, South Africa/Bridgeman Art Library 124, New York Historical Society, New York, USA/Bridgeman Art Library 127,

Lambeth Palace, London, UK/Bridgeman Art Library 137, Fitzwilliam Museum, University of Cambridge, UK/Bridgeman Art Library 141, Philip Mould, Historical Portraits Ltd, London, UK/Bridgeman Art Library 149, Private Collection/Bridgeman Art Library 155, Christie's Images/Bridgeman Art Library 158, Yale Centre for British Art, Paul Mellon Fund, USA/Photo: Bridgeman Art Library 160, Private Collection/Bridgeman Art Library 167, British Library, London, UK/Bridgeman Art Library 169, Private Collection/Philip Mould, Historical Portraits Ltd, London, UK/Bridgeman Art Library 205, National Portrait Gallery, London, UK/Bridgeman Art Library 208, Courtesy of the Trustees of Sir John Soane's Museum, London/Bridgeman Art Library 225, Museé Saint-Denis, Reims, France/Peter Willi/Bridgeman Art Library 230, Dulwich Picture Gallery, London UK/Bridgeman Art Library 244, Courtesy of the Trustees of Sir John Soane's Museum London/Bridgeman Art Library 252, Rafael Valls Gallery, London, UK/Bridgeman Art Library 253, Leeds Museums and Galleries (City Art Gallery) UK/Bridgeman Art Library 254, Southampton City Art Gallery, Hampshire, UK/Bridgeman Art Library 257, Manchester City Art Galleries, UK/Bridgeman Art Library 260, Roy Miles Fine Paintings/Bridgeman Art Library 269, Private Collection/Philip Mould, Historical Portraits Ltd, London, UK/Bridgeman Art Library 277,

The Makins Collection/Bridgeman Art Library 289, Private Collection/Bridgeman Art Library 295, Manchester City Art Galleries, UK/Bridgeman Art Library 310; British Library 132, 159, 164, 249, 280, 284; Folger Shakespeare Library 21, 22–3, 28, 30, 49, 68, 94, 98, 106, 114, 136, 152, 175, 200, 204, 207, 213/242, 241, 250–1, 279, 281; Guildhall Library 87, 99, 178, 224, 245/246, 263, 267; Hulton Getty 7 (bottom), 45/46, 50, 63/81, 88, 147/170, 161, 275, 282–3; Mary Evans Picture Library 4–5/206, 33, 36, 41, 55, 103, 121, 183; Museum of London 44, 102, 188–9; National Maritime Museum 96–7, 150, 156–7, 168; National Portrait Gallery 38, 40, 59, 61, 69, 72, 75, 86, 89, 95, 116, 120, 123, 126, 128, 146, 163, 172, 177, 182, 185, 195, 198, 212, 221, 229, 233, 236, 278, 286, 287, 290; Public Record Office 62, 165, 174; Royal Collection 119, 292–3, 296; Scottish National Portrait Gallery 91; Sotheby's Picture Library 7 (top), 20, 31, 51, 52–3, 56–7, 65, 84, 90, 100, 104–5, 130–1, 133, 134, 142–3, 154, 176, 180, 186, 191, 192, 196–7, 215, 216–17, 218, 222, 226–7, 247, 248, 258–9, 264–5, 300–1, 306–7; Superstock 1; University of Birmingham Collections 234; Victoria & Albert Museum 145, 299

PALATIVM REGIVM IN ANGLIÆ REGNO
Hoc est nusquam